Love's Urgent Longings

Wrestling with belief in today's church

GEOFFREY ROBINSON

johngarrattpublishing

Published in Australia by
John Garratt Publishing
32 Glenvale Crescent
Mulgrave VIC 3170

www.johngarratt.com.au

Edited by Helene Clarke
Designed by Lynne Muir
Cover image: iStockphoto.com

Printed by Kanisius Press, Indonesia

National Library of Australia Cataloguing-in-Publication entry

Robinson, Geoffrey, 1937-
Love's urgent longings : wrestling with belief in today's
church / Geoffrey Robinson.
ISBN: 9781920682217 (pbk.)
Subjects: Robinson, Geoffrey, 1937- Catholic Church—Bishops—
Biography. Faith.
282.092

Contents

3. Longing for Community 73

INTRODUCTION

This book tells the story of my spiritual journey over the last few years since I published a book that criticised the response of the Catholic Church to revelations of sexual abuse and called for a new look at all aspects of the two questions of power and sex within the church.[1]

Responses to the book were sharply divided. On the one hand, the Australian bishops felt the need to issue a public statement criticising the book, and a Roman cardinal and several American bishops told me to turn around and go home again when I visited the United States to speak about these issues.

The Australian bishops have invariably been friendly whenever we have chanced to meet, but I have been left with the feeling that, in the eyes of many of them, I have, according to the image you choose, moved beyond the pale, let the side down, left the club, become an outsider rather than an insider. Several bishops have told me that I am not welcome to speak in their dioceses. In my own diocese I have been progressively cut out of functions a bishop might perform and have had to adjust to my new status.

On the other hand, I have been overwhelmed by the avalanche of positive messages from people who felt that, finally, here was a bishop expressing concerns that they had had in their minds for many years. The Roman cardinal dismissed all these people as "disloyal", but the most obvious fact about them is the very opposite of this. These are people who have been intensely loyal all their lives, but are profoundly dissatisfied with the response of the church to abuse and are convinced that it raises many

---

1 *Confronting Power and Sex in the Catholic Church, Reclaiming the Spirit of Jesus*, John Garratt Publishing, Melbourne, 2007.

questions about both power and sex that will not go away until they have been honestly answered.

The crux of the disagreement between the two sides is that I am convinced that, in responding to abuse, we must unflinchingly study all contributing causes and confront them, even when this leads us to question long-standing practices or teachings of the church. The authorities, on the other hand, would say that the teachings and ancient practices of the church have been solemnly proclaimed by the authority of the pope and may never be questioned, not even in responding to abuse.

Living in this strange world for the past few years, with the official and the popular responses so far apart, has forced me to ask such questions as: Do I really belong in the church? Is there any realistic chance that it will ever change to become the kind of church I could give myself to without reservation? What do I do in the meantime? Should I go before I am pushed? Or do I continue to live in a limbo world?

While these feelings have been heightened by recent events, I must add that they are not new. In my younger days I was given a particular understanding of God, religion and church. There was much that was good and, indeed, beautiful in this understanding, but I have found that a significant part of my life since then has consisted in a long and painful journey away from a number of the ideas that had been implanted in me.

If I may single out two ideas in particular, the first is the idea of the Christian life as consisting overwhelmingly in right behaviour before a judgemental God. It concerns what I have come to call "the God of the high jump". The idea was that I should achieve a high level of right behaviour before God and that, if I worked hard, I would achieve that level, I would clear the bar. The problem was that, any time I did clear the bar, it was immediately put up higher. The ultimate level was how Jesus had acted, and I could never reach that high.

This left me with the pervasive feeling that I was always failing, that there was always a higher level I should have attained, and I do not believe that this was either good psychology or good spirituality.

The second is that of putting rational statements about God before a personal relationship with God, of seeing the most important aspect of faith in the intellectual assent to creeds rather than in a response of love between persons. In that mindset I "had the faith" if I submitted my mind to all the teachings, whether I had a personal relationship with God or not.

Some time ago an Australian bishop was speaking with the pastor of one of the big Pentecostal churches and asked him whether many Catholics attended his services. "Oh yes", he replied, "we get many Catholics. In fact, they make the best converts. They have all this wonderful knowledge about Jesus Christ, and their only problem is that they've never met him." While this is a rather glib statement, it must surely be admitted that there can at times be an uncomfortable degree of truth in it.

So this new book will speak of the personal journey that has taken up most of my adult life, and that has now been brought to some form of crisis or decision by the ambivalent situation I find myself in.

My primary audience will be all the people, both old and young, I have met in the last few years who are greatly upset at the church's response to abuse and are struggling with many things within that church. I shall tell a personal story, but I shall try to do so in dialogue with them.

There is only one conviction in my mind as I begin, and that is that I do not wish to simply reject my past and put nothing in its place. I am now in my seventies, so I feel too old to throw everything out and construct a new building from the foundations up. I do not wish to believe in nothing or only in some vague and uncertain spiritual idea. I do not want to drift wherever the currents of the world around me might carry me. If I must leave something behind, I want to do so only because I have found something of equal value to put in its place. Whatever else, I want this to be a positive book.

I hope that this personal story will have something to say to other people.

1

LONGING FOR SOMETHING DEEPER

What first made me dissatisfied with a religion of rational arguments was the presence of restless, insatiable desires within me. These desires were so strong that I eventually came to realise that I am not a serene person who occasionally becomes restless, but a driven person who only occasionally experiences peace.[2] Whether I have been aware of it or not, my whole life has been taken up with my efforts to respond to these desires within me.

I then came across the opening words of one of the poems of St. John of the Cross, one of the greatest writers of all time on the spiritual life.

One dark night
fired by love's urgent longings
- Ah, the sheer grace -
I went out unseen,
my house being now all stilled.[3]

For him it was the urgent longings of love that were the beginning of all that might be called "spiritual" within us. His words spoke to something deep within me, and in them I found a firm starting point, a certainty on which I could build. If we feel confused, we need to go back to basics, and here, I felt, was a certainty that could underpin my entire journey.

2 See Ronald Rolheiser, *Seeking Spirituality*, Hodder and Stoughton, London, 1998, p.3.
3 These are the opening words of the poem *The Dark Night of the Soul*. See *The Collected Works of John of the Cross*, tr. K. Kavanaugh, ICS Publications, Washington D.C., 1991, p.113.

In this book I shall use the term "spiritual" in the broadest of senses to indicate my strivings to go beneath the more immediate desires within me and respond to the deeper desires that I can find there. In this understanding, there are no high jump bars that God or other people have put in place and that I have an obligation to clear, but there are powerful desires within myself that make me want to rise. The spiritual element in my life then consists in consciously responding to the force of these desires as they move me towards higher goals.

Indeed, the spiritual is my response to the very deepest desires within me. I will be spiritual to the extent that I allow these deepest desires, rather than more immediate ones, to guide my life.

In this first chapter I shall choose seven from among the many powerful desires that I find within myself and see where they might lead me. Only in the following two chapters shall I then look to see to what extent this sense of the spiritual might lead me towards more openly religious ideas.

The Desire for Purpose and Meaning

Who am I? Where do I come from? Where am I going? What is the purpose and meaning of my existence?

For as long as I had a firm understanding of the position I held in the church and the work that was asked of me, I felt I had some answers to these questions. But when I was suddenly seen as an outsider, no longer belonging to the safe world I had until then inhabited, I found myself asking these most basic questions again, for they reflect one of the most profound drives within any human being: the search for meaning. There are few things that so eat away at our sense of dignity and self-worth as a loss of a sense of meaning in life.

In responding to this feeling, I found that I was looking for a sense of meaning that came from something deeper than just belonging to a church.

I saw that, to the big questions of life, some people seem to give an answer as basic as "Making money and enjoying myself" or "Me, what's good for me." These answers are a constant temptation and we never leave them behind, and yet the vast majority of people would instinctively seek something more.

I thought of the goal of "Developing the gifts God and my parents have given me, becoming all I'm capable of being", but this seemed to be too turned in on myself and I knew that any worthwhile goal had to also reach out to others.

There is also a dilemma in all of this. On the one hand, in a world full of fears, I could easily settle for modest goals ("Helping my family to live a good and decent life", "Trying to find, and even give, a little happiness").

On the other hand, there is the danger that in adopting these modest goals I could sell myself short by not looking at my deeper desires. This could lead to a lack of the strong and inspiring spiritual underpinning that could be there for me if only I would seek it.

While I need to avoid high jumps, I feel that, if I really want to respond to the depth of the desires within me, I need to choose goals that will allow these desires to move me beyond my comfort zone towards something higher.

Perhaps the best answer lies in a sense of realism. I feel that I need to answer three questions. The first is: If an objective outsider looked closely at the reality of the life I have been living, what conclusions would that person have to draw about the goals I am seeking? Putting aside my dreams and false ideas about myself, what is my actual day-to-day living saying about the goals I in fact pursue? This would base my answer in reality.

The second question involves listening to the deeper

longings within myself, and asking: What goals do I really want to strive for? How high do I want to aim? In my deepest desires, what sort of person do I want to become?

And this would lead to the third question: What can I realistically do to bridge the gap between the first answer and the second? Just how much do I want to bridge that gap?

Whatever the answers might be that I give, high or low, turning inwards or looking outwards, more or less generous, protecting a comfort-zone or stretching beyond it, the answers I give express an important part of the spiritual dimension of my life.

Some years ago there was a top-level meeting in the city where I live on the subject of illegal drugs. Different people spoke of drugs as a physical or mental health problem, a social problem, a law and order problem or an education problem, but I felt that they were missing an important point in that there was no explicit and public mention of the fact that it might also be a spiritual problem.

And yet, it is when people have no sense of meaning, no satisfying answers to the big questions of life, that things like drugs and even suicide can begin to seem attractive. I do not believe that we will make serious progress against drugs and suicide until we confront this spiritual dimension of the problem.

When the dominant idea in a society seems to be that of turning towards the immediate satisfaction of material desires rather than the slower striving towards deeper desires, the spiritual can easily get lost.

Our society has been good at turning us away from many of the more spiritual values of the past, but it has not been good at replacing them with other values. Many people have rejected values and practices of their childhood but have not replaced them with anything truly satisfying.

I have already said that, whatever else I do, I do not want to go down this path and end up with a vacuum in which I have rejected ideas of the past but not replaced them with ideas and values that genuinely inspire me.

I have made the conscious decision, therefore, that, since my firm starting point is "love's urgent longings", I shall try to seek the goal of always asking, in every new situation I encounter, "What is the most loving thing I can do here?" If I can train myself to ask this question, I will be genuinely seeking the spiritual. Needless to say, I would not always be doing the most loving thing, but at least I would be asking the right question.

This seems to be a genuine attempt to respond to the deeper desires within me. It is not simply a "nice" goal, for I am not speaking of some sentimental love. On the contrary, to do the most loving thing when I am at odds with the official church and calling for major reform involves much thinking, some quite difficult loving, and many hard decisions.

THE DESIRE FOR UNITY

Some time ago I spoke with a nun who had worked for years in a poor village in a developing country and was home on a needed rest leave. She told me that, after a week or so at home, she started to feel disturbed and even angry, and did not at first know why. She then realised that what was making her angry was all the choices that were constantly being forced on her.

If she said "yes" to the simple idea of a sandwich, she was promptly asked whether she wanted white, brown or wholegrain bread, butter or low-fat or low-salt margarine. And these were only the preliminaries to what she wanted on the sandwich and the sauce on top of it. Did she then want coffee or tea, and, if so, Indian, Sri Lankan, Chinese or herbal? Did she want to watch television and, if so, which channel?

She soon felt that there was not a moment of the day when she was not being forced to make choices that had simply not been present in the simple village life. In that village life, she felt that she had some idea of what was truly important in her life, but that at home what was important ran the serious risk of becoming lost in all of these unimportant choices that were taking up so much of her time.

It is only when we have a clear sense of what is central to our life that we have a sense that our life is one whole, as everything else is then judged by this central value and accepted or discarded. Only then do we feel that all the different parts of our life are in harmony with each other, that there is a unity to our life. It was this truth that the nun felt was being threatened by all the choices.

On Christmas Eve of 1992 I had the near-death experience of an emergency coronary bypass. I survived, and came to feel strongly that every moment after that was pure gift, and so a moment that was to be used to the best of my ability.

In coming to terms with this I decided to make a trip to the Sinai Desert in 1994. I had to leave all my belongings at home and bring with me just one suitcase. In Jerusalem I had to leave this suitcase behind and take into the Sinai Desert only what could be carried in a small rucksack. When we left our camp in the desert to climb Mount Sinai, I had to leave even the contents of this rucksack behind me and take only the essentials of water and a few dried figs.

And what I needed to do at the physical level, I found that I also had to do at a deeper level if I truly wanted to use this visit to the Sinai Desert to deepen the spiritual dimension of my life. At this spiritual level I also had to progressively leave baggage behind me in order to come closer to what was most essential, to what gave a sense of unity to my life. I saw why most major religions had begun in desert areas, where such stark choices are forced upon people.

For most of my adult life I have felt rushed, facing too many demands by too many people. I felt that I was constantly being forced to react to other people's needs, demands and desires, and this meant that I was constantly doing what other people thought important rather than what I thought important. This in turn harmed the sense of unity in my life, and the longing for unity became a more powerful desire within me.

Yes, meeting the legitimate needs of other people should be a high priority for me, but the force of demands is not always a good indication of the legitimacy of needs. As a constant practice, responding to the demands of others will leave me with little sense of unity.

Nowadays I know that if someone asks me to do something and I reply, "I'm sorry, I don't have time", what I really mean is that what that person is asking of me is not important enough for me to make time for it. If it were important enough, I would find the time. Often the answer that I don't have time is a perfectly reasonable answer, for we each have the same twenty-four hours in a day, and we have time only for those things that are most important to us.

In deciding what to do with each day I have to have priorities in my life, things for which I will find time. The priorities will vary from person to person – parents must find time for their children, a prime minister must find time to face the major issues of the country, a monk must find time to pray. No one can do everything and meet all the priorities of everyone.

So I, too, must have my priorities, things I will find time for and that give a sense of unity to my life. If I do not, I will find my life fragmented or compartmentalised, with the different parts having little to do with each other and with no sense of unity between them.

It would be easy to give a "pious" answer to the question of what is central to my life, but this book is not about the pious, and it is far too early to bring anything overtly religious into it. At the level of the journey I am seeking to describe, I here need something more basic.

The book that I published in 2007 was, I hope, an invitation to dialogue about issues that I feel need to be looked at again. I hope the book was ultimately about integrity, though that is always something we are striving for rather than something we have already attained. I know that, in the situation in which I now find myself, this striving for integrity has become one of my deepest desires, and hence one of the great unifying forces of my life, one of the first criteria in deciding what I can and can not find time for.

I feel that, if I add the seeking of integrity to the seeking always to do the most loving thing, I will be responding to deeper desires for both meaning and unity, and so I will be seeking the spiritual.

THE DESIRE FOR ENERGY[4]

In order to respond to the insatiable desires within me I want and need energy – physical, mental, emotional and spiritual. So the desire for the maximum possible energy is itself one of the deepest desires with me.

I have come to realise, however, that in responding to this desire for energy, I need to find a balance between two things. I need to foster the greatest possible energy and fire within me and allow it expression, but I also need to have that energy under my control, so that it is not wasted by firing off in every direction. If I want to go to the depth of this desire, it must include the desire for control of energy.

---

4 For this third approach, I am indebted to Ronald Rolheiser, *op.cit.*

If I feel no energy within me, I know that my quest for the spiritual will lack a driving force. But I also know that, if I lack control over how my energy is used, I will fail to attain the goals I desire.

The absence of a dam where one is needed is an absence of energy, so that for large parts of the year the soil is without water and cannot produce a crop. A dam bursting is energy without control, causing death and destruction for all in its path. A dam releasing a controlled amount of water is a source of power through hydroelectricity and of irrigation for the surrounding countryside.

I have to find a balance, a creative tension, between order and chaos. Too much order (over-control) and I would suffocate, too much chaos (lack of control) and my energy would be wasted. If I do not get the balance right, I know that I can fluctuate between being out of touch with the source of energy (apathy) and not being able to control it (restlessness).

In earlier times people were aware of the harm energy can do, so they surrounded it with prohibitions and rituals, especially in the fields of sex and religion. Sex was surrounded by so many prohibitions that the dominant outlook was frequently negative, emphasising dangers and prohibitions, rather than positive, emphasising creativity and potential for good. In so far as religion was seen in terms of right behaviour before a judgemental God, it too was presented in overly negative terms.

In both cases the tendency was to see everything in terms of right and wrong actions rather than in the positive terms of relationships with others, including God.

All too often this tendency ran the danger of becoming a path of fear and prohibition, stifling the energy itself. This may have given a certain social stability, but ultimately it was the taking away of necessary energy from both individuals and entire communities, so that they could not grow as they should.

Today there has been a widespread reaction against these prohibitions. In many people this tendency has been a sign of growing maturity that has greatly enhanced their ability to grow. Their reaction against many religious restrictions has been a perfectly correct one, and for most of my adult life I have instinctively been part of this reaction and it has been an important part of the journey of my adult life.

On the other hand, I do not want to react against one extreme simply by going to the opposite extreme. I do not want to react against excess of control by moving to lack of control. In reacting against all the restrictions on sex, I do not want to go to the opposite extreme of no restrictions or control, for that would inevitably harm both other people and myself. In reacting against the restrictions of a negative religious attitude, I do not want to abandon everything that is of value in my religious tradition.

In both cases I want to find a middle way based on relationships and on love. Much of my earlier book involved the attempt to do precisely this in relation to both power and sex within the Catholic Church.

Fire and water have always been important in spiritual symbolism. Fire symbolises energy and passion, water symbolises a cooling down, a holding in containment, a conscious directing of my energy to useful purposes. In my spiritual life I am forever in a forge, heated and shaped by fire, then cooled by water. Good laws and structures in a community can be of some assistance in finding the right balance, but ultimately it is only within myself that a true balance can be found.

In my own life I would have to confess that lessons learned about the control of energy have frequently prevented me from accessing the full energy I might have had. I have, therefore, made the conscious decision to seek the greatest degree of the fire of energy that I can cope with and intelligently use. I feel that, if I can do this, I will be a more spiritual person.

THE DESIRE FOR FREEDOM

Freedom is essential to all my desires, for it is the basis of my autonomy, my being in charge of my own life, my being able to take responsibility for my decisions, and hence to grow to become all I am capable of being. It is an essential basis of my attempt to rise towards higher goals.

I do not speak only of freedom from physical force, but also of freedom from harmful ideas or influences. For example, on my personal journey I had to learn freedom from the God of the high jump before I could truly respond to the desires within me. I had to learn freedom from the idea of faith as intellectual assent to creeds before I could truly develop a faith of response of love to love.

Even this is not enough, for it is still a negative freedom – freedom from negative forces. To take the desire for freedom to its depths, I must think in terms of positive freedom, the freedom to do things.

Occasionally, people in prison have produced masterworks of literature or art, that is, while lacking negative freedom, they were able to use the opportunity and the resources within themselves to produce something of great worth. Despite the prison and its lack of negative freedom, they had a genuine positive freedom.

On the other hand, there can be people today for whom negative freedom seems to be an absolute value, who cast off all restraints and reject the advice of all other people, but because of a lack of knowledge and resources within themselves, lack the positive freedom to achieve anything worthwhile with their lives.

Who is more genuinely free: the person in prison producing a great work of literature or the person outside prison who does not know how to achieve anything of value?

It could never be enough for me to reject the idea of the God of the high jump or the idea of faith as intellectual assent to creeds if the rejection simply left me with belief in nothing, for that would be merely negative freedom. It would only be through a genuine effort to respond to the desires within myself and build a life of relationships that I would begin to find positive freedom.

Now that I am retired, I find that I have a good degree of negative freedom from the demands of other people, so my conscious decision is to seek the maximum degree of positive freedom, especially in the fields of responding to the deeper desires within myself and in building relationships.

The Desire for Happiness

The "pursuit of happiness" is a universal goal and it touches things so deep within me that it, too, is a significant part of my search for the spiritual.

And yet happiness is an elusive concept. I know that a meal with friends or a holiday might make me happy, but I can't always be out with friends or on holiday. Winning the lottery might make me happy, but I suspect that the happiness would not last, for it would not touch my deeper longings.

Today there is much uncertainty about the future, and there is a culture all around me that seeks to turn my eyes away from this anxiety-provoking future by constantly inviting me to lose myself in the pleasures of the moment, even though I know that lasting happiness is not to be found there.

There is happiness when, after much hard work, I finally achieve some goal I have been striving for. There is happiness when I am able to offer significant help to someone who needs me. And there is happiness when I feel that, by coming through some difficulty, I have been able to become a better person. But even these desirable feelings cannot be with me all the time.

One writer suggests that the problem is that, though I desire happiness so much, I cannot really pursue it directly.[5] He says that, if I want to find a happiness deeper than the present moment, it must be the by-product of seeking deeper things in my life, and he condenses this into ten life-tasks. He says that they are not simple tasks that can be done once and for all, but genuine life-tasks. The more I accomplish these life-tasks, the more I will attain a deeper happiness and a genuine spirituality.

1. I must learn to accept myself as I am. Self-liking people are at peace with themselves and free to move out towards others, self-hating people are not.

2. I must accept full responsibility for my life, for growth begins only where blaming others ends.

3. I must try to fulfil my needs for relaxation, exercise and nourishment.

4. I must make my life an act of love. Most people have a question that they instinctively ask in each new situation. It might be, "How can I make the most money here" or "How can I have the most fun", or any of a hundred other questions. In pursuing true happiness, he suggests that the best question is the one I have already mentioned, "What is the most loving thing to do here?"

5. I must stretch myself by stepping out of my comfort zone.

---

5 John Powell SJ, *Happiness is an Inside Job*, Tabor Publishing, Valencia, California, 1989. What follows is taken from this book.

6. Without being naïve, I must learn to look for what is good in myself, in others and in the world around me rather than concentrate all the time on the negatives. A study of one hundred happy people found that this simple attitude was what contributed most to their sense of happiness.
7. While I seek growth, I must not set up impossible standards and feel a failure if I do not achieve them.
8. I must learn to communicate as effectively as possible, for "we are as sick as we are secret", and I will be healthy and happy when I can give freely and receive gracefully.
9. While avoiding excess, I must learn to enjoy the good things of life.
10. I must daily and consciously seek the spiritual in my life and in the world around me.

Obviously I am free to add to this list, subtract from it or change it, but it surely tells me that seeking a deep and lasting happiness and seeking higher goals are one and the same thing.

The struggle for a happiness so deep that it would be untouched by external events is another of the conscious and deeper goals that I would like to set for myself.

THE DESIRE FOR PEACE

I have lived a busy life, surrounded by countless demands on my time and attention. Constantly I longed for moments when I could get away from these demands and "find some peace".

When I retired, however, I found that the taking away of many of the demands did not bring the peace I hoped for. Indeed, I discovered that I can no more find lasting peace in the absence of all activity than I can find lasting happiness in being always at a party. Paradoxically, I quickly found that, in order to be at peace, I needed to keep busy.

There is a common misunderstanding that things are peaceful when nothing is happening. The most famous definition of peace, however, is that of St. Augustine, who said that it is "the tranquillity of order". He was referring particularly to peace as gift when order is grounded in God's will, but I believe that the idea has a wider application.

In human affairs order is not a passive concept, where nothing is happening, but an active concept, where many things are happening, but are happening "in order".

A plane in flight looks peaceful, but it will remain peaceful only for as long as the driving force of the engines pushes it forwards. If the engines cease to push it, that is, if nothing happens, the peace would quickly be shattered.

Far from being the simple absence of things happening, international peace is a very complex notion. It demands that many things be happening, and requires constant thought and attention by many people. It demands, for example, that aid be rushed to those in desperate need, that refugees be cared for, that nations not be saddled with impossible debts, that trade and development be assisted, that good governance be demanded and that the causes of tension be dealt with resolutely and as early as possible. It demands the highest possible level of active order in international affairs.

In my own life, too, a true sense of peace needs to be based on many things happening, but happening "in order". Even in terms of things already mentioned in this chapter, it demands that I have a sense of meaning and unity, a proper balance between energy and control of energy and a movement towards a deeper sense of happiness. If none of these things were happening, it would be impossible for me to be "at peace".

Honesty demands that I add that there have been many

moments over the past few years when I devoutly wished that I had not written a book that would arouse such opposition, for it has certainly harmed my peace. But then I had to ask where true peace is to be found - in remaining silent or in saying things that I believe are essential to genuine order. So my quest for deeper peace has become a searching for peace in turmoil, a longing and struggling for an order that is based on justice, love and integrity. I feel that, if I work hard for that kind of peace, I will truly be seeking the spiritual.

THE DESIRE FOR LOVE

The deepest longing of my heart is the longing for love, for it comes from the very centre of my being. All my other desires and longings, including the six I have just spoken of, can be traced back to this source and are simply different expressions of this one fundamental longing. It is so deep that nothing on this earth can satisfy it, not even all the loves of my life put together.

Whenever I try to say anything about this longing in words, however, I find that I ask too much of the poor little word "love". The ancient Greeks at least came closer by having three words to express three different aspects of love: *eros* (desire), *philia* (affection) and *agape* (self-giving love).[6]

Since the time of Freud, *eros* and its adjective "erotic" have been largely restricted to sexual desire, but in earlier times the word included all desire. *Eros* or desire is the unquiet aspect of love, what Rolheiser describes as the fire within, the

6 There is, in fact, some variety in the way the words are used in the Second Testament and what I say here is admittedly a simplification. See *Theological Dictionary of the New Testament*, edited by Gerhard Kittel and Gerhard Friedrich, translated and abridged in one volume by Geoffrey W. Bromley, William B Erdmans Publishing, Grand Rapids, 1985.

restlessness, the loneliness and nostalgia for better times, the wildness and ache at the centre of my being. It can be felt as a pain, dissatisfaction and frustration, but it can also be felt as an energy and pull towards beauty and creativity. It is a subject of eternal fascination, so stories about desire, sexual attraction, journeys into the unknown, tragic loss and triumphant regaining have always been popular.[7]

I can desire something with all my being and yet, when I achieve it, find that it has done little to assuage the deepest desires of my heart. Ultimately, all desire, no matter what form it takes, is a desire for the other two forms of love, *philia* and *agape*.

Philia is the affection that I feel for those close to me. I want them to be an important part of my life, I want all that is good for them, and I want these two things so much that strong feelings are spontaneously engaged. *Philia* can include all the feelings of romantic love and all the tenderness of true friendship.

Agape is the love that goes out to others without looking for anything for myself. It is the genuine love I might feel for people on the far side of the world who are dying of hunger. It does not exclude affection (e.g. the self-giving love of parents), but it extends even to people for whom I have no feelings of love. It is the type of love that can be known only from the actions it prompts and, if it prompted no actions in me, others would rightly conclude that I did not possess it.

It exists within all people who have not totally hardened themselves to others. If some self-sacrifice would prevent a war between two countries, I hope that I would be willing to make that sacrifice. Even if the condition were attached that no one would ever learn of the sacrifice, I hope that I would still act.

All true love starts as desire, leads to affection, and then rises to self-giving love. For example, a couple desire a child

---

7 See Ronald Rolheiser, *op. cit.*, p.4.

(*eros*), are overwhelmed by feelings of affection and tenderness when they first hold their baby in their arms (*philia*), but, the very first night they bring the child home from the hospital, quickly discover that in practice this love means immense self-giving (*agape*).

Religion can make the mistake of seeing this process in terms of a line moving upwards, in which self-giving love is the higher love, and desire and affection are left behind. But the process should be a circle, not a straight line, for it is important that self-giving should not leave desire and affection behind, but be constantly strengthened and renewed by them.[8]

My whole life is a response to this multi-faceted longing for love within the depths of my being, and the response to love is the spiritual dimension of my life.

To take a simple example, a young girl might fall in love with the violin and work hard to learn to play it. This love will give her three things. Firstly, it will give a sense of achievement in doing something worthwhile and through this a sense of deeper love, and hence of <u>meaning</u>. Secondly, because it gives a sense of meaning, it will also give the <u>energy</u> to keep on pursuing the love, so that she will continue to work hard to master the instrument. Thirdly, at a later point the love can actually create a significant part of her very <u>identity</u>, so that, if you asked another person "Who is that?", the answer might well be, "Oh, that's the violinist."

The love has then become at least part of her answer to the big questions of life, a feeling that part of the reason for her very existence is to be a carrier of the beauty that violin music can contain.

In the same way, other people become lovers of husband/

---

8 Much beautiful writing on this topic is found in Pope Benedict XVI's encyclical *Deus Caritas Est*, 25th December 2005.

wife and children, lovers of nature, science, literature, animals, sports or an almost infinite variety of other things.

The object of our love can be
— any <u>person</u> such as a husband or wife, a child or a friend;
— any <u>object</u> such as an animal, a flower, a painting or a gemstone;
— any <u>activity</u> such as playing or listening to music, walking by the sea or studying history;
— any <u>idea</u> such as a passion for justice or a search for perfect beauty.

The spiritual dimension of our life then comes from the <u>sum total</u> of the loves of our life. The more genuine love there is in our lives, the more spiritual we are.

There are three conditions. Firstly, the love should give people and things the freedom to grow. It should not be the possessive love that suffocates, the conditional love that manipulates, or the selfish love that seeks only one's own good. It should not be the mistaken love that denies one's own deepest good, for all genuine love should benefit two people, the lover as well as the beloved. Love is not an ability, but a capacity, for it consists in creating space in which people and things are free to grow.[9] If love does not create the freedom to grow, it is not true love.

Secondly, if it is to give meaning and energy, the love should in some manner be returned. Flowers return our love, just by being beautiful, even though they will wither and die. Activities can return the love we give them, though they can also give us bad days when we feel that our love is not returned. A passion for justice can bring much frustration, but it can also bring a powerful return of love. Persons are by far the most satisfying, for no object or activity can return love in the way they can,

9 Gerald G May M.D., *The Awakened Heart*, HarperCollins, San Francisco, 1991, p.10.

though they are also the most dangerous, for no object or activity can hurt in the way they can.

Thirdly, there should be some balance and proportion among the things we love. If the young girl I mentioned earlier spent so much time practising the violin that there was no time left over for people, the love would have become an obsession that would suffocate rather than allow to grow.

There are many paradoxes in love. If I want to see my love returned, I should give without thought of return. Love is not bought or sold, it is always gift. It is fallen into rather than planned. The more I love another person, or even a thing, the more I will make myself vulnerable to be hurt by that person or thing. And yet, despite these paradoxes, it is love alone that gives meaning to my life.

The fragility of love reminds us that we should never take it for granted. On one occasion when I visited a refuge for homeless youths, there was a young man there who had had to appear in court that morning on a charge. I noticed something moving on his upper arm and asked what it was. He unzipped a pocket there and took out his pet mouse. I asked whether he had had the mouse with him in court and he said that he had.

My first thought was that this was a dangerous thing to do, but I then thought that, if a pet mouse is one of the few things in life you love, if it is one of the very few reasons you have for getting up in the morning, then you will insist on keeping it with you in all circumstances. It was a reminder that, after all the talk about love, many people do not find love everywhere they look and have to take the little they can get.

The world of today has destroyed many of the values of the past. At times it presents to me things so grossly superficial that they cannot possibly provide lasting satisfaction. My search for love and meaning is constant, profound, and at times even desperate. I can never take love for granted, and it is good to be grateful for the love that I have in my life. It is love before all else that makes me want to rise above my present situation towards higher goals, for there is never a moment when I do not want more love in my life.

BRINGING THE DESIRES TOGETHER

Can these various desires be brought into one? I believe they can, and the indications are to be found in two things I have already said. In speaking of a girl learning to play the violin, I said that the sense of meaning and satisfaction given by making progress gave the energy to keep on practising and making further progress. In its simplest terms, it was love that created energy. In mentioning the great mystic, John of the Cross, I referred to the same idea, for the energy he presented as the basis of the entire spiritual life was that of "love's urgent longings."

The starting point for the spiritual in my life, and for any spiritual search I undertake, is the insatiable longing for love in the most profound depths of my heart. This longing is so deep and so powerful that it determines every decision I ever make, every action I perform. And all my longings for meaning, unity, energy, freedom, happiness and peace are nothing more than expressions of this most basic longing for love.

This deep longing for love is the firmest basis I know for all that I call spiritual in my life. To the extent that I keep striving to respond to the depth of this longing, I will be a spiritual person.

GOOD DESIRES TAKEN TOO FAR

A caution needs to be added. There was once talk of the "seven deadly sins": pride, avarice, lust, gluttony, anger, jealousy, sloth. They were called "deadly" because all other sins could be reduced to one of these seven.

And yet a proper pride in self is essential if I am to reach out to help others, I need money in order to live, it is perfectly legitimate to desire a sexual relationship, I must have necessary food and drink, it is legitimate to defend myself against unjust attacks, it is good to aspire to levels that others have reached and I need to protect my limited resources.

It is only when these legitimate desires are taken too far that they become wrong. Thus pride is a proper self-esteem taken too far, avarice puts the desire for money and material possessions before all other values, lust is the desire for sexual pleasure without concern for others, gluttony is the desire for necessary food taken too far, the sin of anger is the out-of-proportion defence of self, jealousy is substituting the desire to rise to the level of others with the desire to bring them down to my level, and sloth is taking too far the desire not to wear out my limited resources.

It is always the inordinate desire, the wanting "too much" or "too far", that leads me astray, for in themselves the seven things desired are morally and spiritually good. Indeed, because these seven things are legitimate, I must be careful that my attitude towards them never places control of energy above access to legitimate energy. It was this danger of placing the emphasis in the wrong place and stifling energy that has caused the phrase "the seven deadly sins" to fall into disuse. I can use these seven things to help people, and this means that, when I use them in the right way, I can grow spiritually through them.

Despite this, each of these seven desires can be taken too far. Pride can tempt me to power and authority for their own sake, rather than in order to help others. I do not wish to be rich, and yet I always seem to want more money than I have, and I notice that even the richest people do that. I cannot deny the temptation to sex without love and to using people for my own satisfaction. I know how easy it is to eat or drink more than is good for me. It is not easy to be assertive without becoming aggressive. It is hard to rise to the level of others, and it can be easier to attempt to drag them down to my level. And the desire not to do too much can easily become the desire to do too little.

In the same way, even the seven good desires I have spoken about as fundamental to the spiritual life can be distorted and taken too far. I have seen all seven as expressions of the deepest desire of all, the desire for love, and yet even love can go astray and I can love the wrong things.

> Love cannot be idle. What is it that moves absolutely any person, even to do evil, if it is not love? Show me a love that is idle and doing nothing. Scandals, adulteries, crimes, murders, every kind of excess, are they not the work of love? Cleanse your love, then. Direct into the garden the water that was running down the drain. Am I telling you not to love anything? Far from it! If you do not love anything you will be dolts, dead persons, despicable creatures. Love, by all means, but take care what it is you love. [10]

To all that has been said in this chapter, therefore, it is important to add that it is not enough to desire. The fire of my desires must be tempered by the water of control, so that I love the right things, seek peace in the existence of true order rather than in doing nothing, work for positive freedom rather than merely insist on unlimited negative freedom, and seek a deeper happiness rather than be lost in immediate pleasures. The more I can go beneath the surface and become in touch with the very deepest desires within me, the more spiritual I will be.

---

10 St. Augustine, Sermon II on the Psalms, 31:5.

And good desire requires intelligence just as much as any other activity in my life.

It may help me to remain on the right path if I remind myself of the seven deadly social sins of which Mahatma Gandhi spoke: politics without principle, wealth without work, commerce without morality, pleasure without conscience, education without character, science without humanity, and worship without sacrifice.

2

LONGING FOR PERFECT LOVE

In the first chapter I started from the desires within myself and tried to see whether they could lead me to a satisfying sense of the spiritual in my life. Now I must see whether this sense of the spiritual needs to include the idea of God.

It may surprise some people that a bishop asks questions about the very existence of God, but I believe that all people need to ask them, for not to ask them runs the risk of a faith that puts a coat of paint over doubts rather than confronts them. This would seriously harm any form of spiritual life. Since my response to the situation I find myself in is to go back to basics, I feel that I need to look at this question again with fresh eyes.

There are real questions that demand honest answers. Indeed, these questions are so basic that at times they appear to face me with an impossible choice between, on the one hand, a god who allows evil and suffering, and, on the other, a world without meaning. And that should never be an easy choice for any human being who has both a heart and a head.

Furthermore, in today's world people who turn away from the church will, sooner rather than later, find their belief in the very existence of God challenged. If such people are to be part of the dialogue of this book, I cannot ignore the questions that this challenge presents for them.

To Fly Beyond the Stars

My starting point is once again the desires within me, especially the desire for love.

My sense of love comes, above and before all else, from my

relationships with those closest to me, for nothing can take their place and without them my life would be poor indeed. I also gain much from the feelings of goodwill, friendship and love that come to me from all the people I work with or meet, for most people at most times are friendly, honest and compassionate.

My sense of love then comes from a wide variety of objects, activities and ideas: from the marvellous complexity of nature, from stars and planets, and atoms and particles; from the fluid grace of a horse or cheetah or eagle or dolphin; from music and dance and poetry; from a passion for justice for the poorest people in the world and a desire for reconciliation with the dispossessed. Not least, it also comes from every circumstance where I find a response to any of the longings I have spoken of.

It comes from all these things and many more, and even then it has always left me with a profound sense that all these loves are not enough, that there must be something more.

Every time I experience love for anything at all, I feel some satisfaction and sense of meaning in my life, but I also know that I long for a deeper and fuller love and meaning. I feel that I am somehow a prisoner within my body and I long to escape and fly beyond the stars. My longings can never be fully satisfied, for ultimately I long for perfect love and perfect meaning. Any understanding of life that does not even attempt to speak to this almost infinite longing will not satisfy me.

It is the very depth, the almost infinity, of the longing for love within me that has led me to believe that there will always be something missing at the centre of my life unless I can find a love so great that it needs the word "divine" attached to it. Without this "divine" love, I feel that there is always the danger that I will ask too much of objects and persons in this world.

Music can express exquisite beauty, but I know that I cannot demand total meaning of the whole of life from music. Romantic love is overwhelmingly beautiful, but I know that it would be dangerous to demand total meaning in life forever from one other limited person. I feel that this something called "divine love" alone could meet the bottomless depth of my longing for love.

I know that my longing for divine love does not prove its existence, for I can long with all my soul for the pot of gold at the end of the rainbow, and that does not mean that there is one there. The longing for infinite love does, however, explain why I have felt the attraction of some form of belief in the divine.

In dealing with this attraction, I felt that I needed to come to terms with something of the story of belief and unbelief over the last few centuries. It is here that rational thinking cannot be ignored, and I ask indulgence as I consider these issues over the next few pages before returning to my personal story.

Four Body Blows

I must start by acknowledging that the nineteenth century dealt four serious body blows to religion, and we are still living in the deep shadow of these four forces.

The first was that the work of Charles Darwin took away many of the arguments used by religious authorities for an active divine presence in the world and seemed to relegate God to a more distant sphere. It was realised that much of what had formerly been attributed directly to God must rather be attributed to forces in nature, so that large quantities of religious literature and many arguments drawn from the Bible were discredited. The famous statement of Archbishop James Ussher that the earth was created at midday on 23rd October 4004 B.C.E. quickly became an oft-repeated joke.

Darwin's work did not prove the non-existence of God, for it still allowed for the idea that the forces in nature came ultimately from God. But it undoubtedly undermined many traditional religious arguments and so had the effect of creating a world in which it was easier to be an unbeliever than it had been. For reasons that go well beyond Darwin, the strong social support for religious belief, which had until that time greatly assisted religion, was also undermined, so that belief began to become the very personal choice it remains today.

The second body blow came from critical study of the Bible, for this destroyed the more literal understanding of the Bible that had become popular, and the battle between scientific study and fundamentalism still continues today.[11] It has become quite impossible, for example, to believe that the world was created in six days, and those who continue to hold to such beliefs have become figures of ridicule. The Scopes "monkey" trial of 1925 is still seen by many as the great clash of these two forces and the definitive victory for science over religion.[12]

The third body blow was that, in the battle during that century between what seemed to be a fresh science and a tired religion, science began to win more and more of the crucial battles for the imagination of people. To many it seemed that science held out a more exciting vision for the future of humankind, and they turned to this vision. "Religions die when their lights fail",[13] when they no longer speak to the concerns of the people, when they no longer fire the imagination. In the battle between reason and faith, reason seemed to be winning decisively the battle for the imagination, at least in the Western world.

---

11 See Karen Armstrong, *The Battle for God, Fundamentalism in Judaism, Christianity and Islam,* Harper Perennial, London, 2000.
12 John Scopes, a young teacher in Tennessee was brought to trial for teaching evolution in a public school. The rationalist lawyer Clarence Darrow routed and destroyed his opponent William Jennings Bryan by showing the contradictions that a literal reading of the Bible on this subject leads to.
13 Wolfhart Pannenberg.

The fourth blow also had its origins in the nineteenth century, though it did not appear until later. In the Industrial Revolution many people were oppressed in the name of "progress". What was seen as the good of society was put before the good of the individual, and, indeed, the individual was sacrificed to society. In the reaction against this in the 1960s, of which I shall speak later in this book, the roles were reversed, the individual was put above society, and individualism became powerful. Those who insist on being the centre of their own universe will always be strongly driven to reject the idea of God, for there cannot be two centres. Belief in God will then be seen as taking away from human dignity and autonomy. Religion, on the other hand, is essentially about community and will always be battling up a steep hill in a world where individualism reigns supreme.

Any knowledge we may have of God can come from only two sources: the world around and within us, and the stories of God's dealings with the world handed down from earlier times. But if God is not immediately present in every action around us, if a literal reading of the Bible has had to take so many steps backwards, if the extraordinary advances in science so appeal to the imagination, and if individualism reigns, there is little wonder that religion still experiences massive difficulties.

The result is that today belief in God has become a very personal thing, and little can be taken for granted.

Belief and Unbelief

In the great debates over belief and unbelief that took place in that same nineteenth century, various thinkers took up an idea of the philosopher Immanuel Kant. They said that there are no scientific proofs, either of God's existence or of God's non-existence, and by scientific proofs they meant proofs that are so grounded in observable evidence and so cogent that any fair-minded person would have no choice but to accept them. They concluded that religious faith and atheism are equally acts of <u>faith</u> rather than of reason, for each is the free choice of something that lies beyond scientific proof. This is the view I have come to share.

In my student days I studied some of the works of a great thinker, St. Thomas Aquinas. He did not speak of scientific, but of philosophical proofs of the existence of God. He argued that there must be a first cause of all that exists, a purposeful and intelligent designer of the order of creation, a necessary cause of all the contingent things that exist, a first mover of all things that move, and a perfection against which all beauty, truth and goodness can be measured.

I have over the years had increasing problems with these arguments, for they seem to stop a long way short of a god with whom I could actually have a personal relationship. They leave the question of evil and suffering untouched, such that I have to ask what kind of first cause or prime mover these arguments speak about. Very few people come to the question of God out of philosophical conviction; they come because of the profound longings within themselves, especially the longing for love, and an impersonal first cause or prime mover does not speak to these longings. Such arguments would never win the crucial battle for the imagination.

On the other hand, I was also disappointed with the arguments of opponents of belief such as Feuerbach, Marx, Nietzscke and Freud. They said that God is nothing more than a human invention, a projection of the human longing for security. I felt that, if we are to argue in this manner, we might reply with equal validity that that other act of faith, atheism, is nothing more than a projection of the human longing for autonomy. I felt that it remains true that there are no real proofs on either side.

Over the course of the same nineteenth century science exploded and it was increasingly said that we should not believe anything unless we have positive and scientific proof, so in the absence of positive proof of the existence of God we should be atheists. The same argument is propounded by many of the modern militant atheists, and the idea is at the heart of today's often heated debate between belief and unbelief.

I feel that the problem arises from the very success of science over the last two hundred years. This success was achieved through the rigorous application of the scientific method of hypothesis and dispassionate experiment. The method was so brilliantly successful, and produced such astounding results, that many concluded that it was the only way in which to study any subject at all, and its findings were the only findings that should be accepted. Anything that was not the result of scientific method was mere "myth" and was to be rejected. This idea gained widespread acceptance and is one of the dominant ideas in the modern world.

The difficulty with the argument is that not everything can be subjected to such scientific experiment. Art, music, literature, love, kindness and gentleness are obvious examples of things that cannot be placed under a microscope in a laboratory, and yet have their important place in our lives. The desires I spoke about in the first chapter also come into this category, and I feel that it is a pointless waste of time for anyone to tell me that I must ignore these deepest longings of my heart simply because they are not sufficiently open to scientific study.

In relation to belief in the divine, the best model is possibly that of history. From a serious historian I ask two things. Firstly, I ask a truly scientific approach in which, with full scientific rigour, as much information as possible about a particular period or event in history is carefully and systematically gathered, sifted, marshalled and then expressed in a form that quotes sources and makes a sharp distinction between what is proven fact and what is not.

But I then want more than this. I want the historian to use all the knowledge gained to enter into the minds and hearts of the people of that time and place, to think with their thoughts, to feel with their feelings, to make me believe that I am there in the middle of them, sharing both their hopes and their fears. In this second element it will not always be possible to proceed according to full scientific method, for at this point there must be room for imagination, intuition and empathy. And yet without this second less scientific element I fear that the history would be arid, soulless and all too inclined to put students to sleep in class.

Yes, there is a great difference between history according to the strictest scientific criteria, and a novel or film loosely based on historical events, but there is much room between the two.

In studying belief in the divine I want the same two elements. I feel no attraction to any form of fundamentalism that demands a literal reading of the words of the Bible and rejects the idea of serious, scientific study of everything within the world of the Bible that can be subjected to such study. I welcome all those scientific studies of geography, history and especially archaeology that have led to a deeper understanding of the cultures, languages, laws and customs of the people of the Bible.

I admire the integrity of those scholars who began their archaeological excavations confident that they would support the historical accuracy of the Bible concerning the coming into the Promised Land of the people of Israel, but when they did not, immediately published their findings and revised their own ideas.

The discoveries concerning the Bible have been so great that over my lifetime I have had to revise many of my understandings of what the Bible contains. In particular, I have learned to distinguish between fact and prose on the one hand, and the wealth of poetry, story, symbol and parable on the other. I have come to understand that many things that I once considered hard fact are instead invented stories meant to bring out the religious truth in an underlying fact – "myths" in the true sense of that word.

I have had to grapple with the fact that, in a manner quite foreign to modern Western thinking, historians of earlier times placed far greater emphasis on the meaning of events than on the details of the events themselves, and would indeed feel quite free to change the details in order to bring out the meaning.

In seeking to understand all that the Bible contains, however, I also need to go beyond this scientific study. I want to enter into the story and walk with the Israelites as they leave behind slavery in Egypt and gradually and painfully work their way towards a new religious understanding. I want to somehow be present and feel the full force of the personality of Jesus as he walks the roads of Galilee and moves towards his mission in Jerusalem.

I want the great stories or myths of the Bible to be part of my life, for it is those stories that can give me a sense of meaning in life in a way that science alone can not. Belief in the divine belongs with art, love and history rather than in a laboratory.

FAITH, REASON AND FEELINGS

There is a further factor. While the battle between faith and reason still continues today, the important new fact is that it may be in the process of being superseded. When two forces fight each other over a long period, there is always the danger that outsiders will eventually reject both of them.

This may actually be happening in so far as today it is

often <u>feelings</u> that are in battle against both faith and reason. Feelings will never completely banish either faith or reason, but they have unquestionably become a third force to be reckoned with, and the movement towards feelings has attracted many followers.

With the benefit of hindsight, we can see that the arguments of the proponents of reason were often too coldly rational, and did not take sufficient account of feelings. In the attempt to combat the proponents of reason, the defenders of faith could also become too rational, forgetting their feelings, and leading to a religion where intellectual assent to propositions came before personal relationships.

So today we see a movement in which, for many people in the Western world, feelings are increasingly taking the place of both reason and faith. Many people do not trust religious faith and have also lost much of their trust in cold scientific reason. Instead, they place their trust in their own feelings as a guide for their lives.

There is certainly a truth here. We are not computers, but human beings who feel as well as think. We cannot ignore our feelings without leaving out a most important part of who and what we are. Psychology would teach us that frequently our feelings are the major path into an understanding of the important world of the subconscious that determines so much of what we think and say and do. The addition of feelings to faith and reason is an important step forward.

At the same time, there has been a tendency to see feelings as completely replacing faith and reason rather than being combined with them, and this has introduced its own difficulties into the modern world.

In responding to this, it is essential to do more than simply condemn relativism, subjectivism, hedonism, individualism and a whole list of other related "isms" that can go with a world based on feelings. The constant condemnation of all these "isms" is a negative policy that is most unlikely to achieve positive results.

This essential task is the more difficult one of appreciating the importance of all three elements, and working hard towards a proper and positive synthesis of faith, reason and feelings in my life. I absolutely do not want my faith to tell me one thing, my reason another and my feelings a third. I must recognise that each is supreme within its own field, and I need to bring them together and harmonise them. This will be a serious task, both for me personally and for the entire Western world, but I believe it is the way into a better future.

> ... being Christian is not simply to be a person who subscribes to a set of beliefs or facts, though Christianity most certainly requires attention to what is true or false, to what is or is not the case... Being Christian, however, engages imagination and emotion, energy and passion, not as an 'extra' to belief, but as integral, central to it. And we might inhabit our tradition with greater ease if we learned to give emotion and imagination greater weight as we try to find our way about in it. For if these dimensions of our lives are not engaged, can we effectively and seriously believe in any case?[14]

PERSONAL EXPERIENCE AND PERSONAL PREFERENCE

To return now to my personal story, I accept that there are no scientific proofs of either God's existence or God's non-existence; there are only indications pointing towards God's existence and indications pointing towards God's non-existence, and I must balance these indications against each other.   ·

---

14 Anne Loades, "Word and Sacrament: Recovering Integrity" in Neil Brown and Robert Gascoigne (ed), *Faith in the Public Forum*, Adelaide: Australian Theological Forum, 1998, p.30.

Precisely because of the absence of scientific proofs, the number of people in the world who make their decision in favour of either atheism or religious belief on the basis of pure philosophical argument or strict scientific evidence is probably very small.

I suggest that whether a person chooses belief or unbelief will probably depend far more on two other factors that go together: the personal experience of the individual, and what that person wants to believe.

It will depend on experience because it is an important psychological fact that people always react with their feelings before they react with their minds, and it is only when they get their emotional response right that they will give an adequate intellectual response. And their feelings depend far more on personal experience than on rational arguments.

Indeed, if an argument between two people comes to an impasse, the best way to take the matter forward is usually for each of the two to take the time to learn something of the other's personal story, for this will tell them why they believe what they do. This truth certainly applies to any argument concerning religious belief.

For example, in trying hard to be a good monk, Martin Luther was tormented by what he saw as the impossibility of constant right action before a judgemental God, and developed his ideas on justification by faith alone as a response to this. It is a sad fact that, if only, instead of issuing condemnations, someone from Rome had actually taken the trouble to sit down with Luther and really listen to his personal story, the Reformation may have taken a different course.

The decision between belief and unbelief will also depend on what people want to believe, for often it is feelings that lead reason rather than reason leading feelings, with people then believing what they want to believe.

Thus one person might, at a time of great personal turmoil,

be befriended by a religious neighbour, and be so moved by this that it determines their emotional response to religion, with their intellectual response following behind, and the heart leading the head towards belief. Another person might have a bad experience within a religious body, and walk away with the powerful emotional determination to reject everything that "they" stand for, with the heart leading the head to unbelief.

It is in this sense that the desire for security can create religious belief and the desire for autonomy can create atheist belief.

Am I saying that any decision between belief and unbelief is purely subjective, or even arbitrary? No. I am simply trying to combine reason and feelings, and to suggest that my rational thinking will always take place against the background of my own personal experience, and those forces within me that lead me to desire certain things and reject certain others. I am suggesting that it is quite impossible to ignore these factors and leave them out of consideration.

I can argue with a person's ideas, but I cannot argue with their psychological needs, and it is these needs rather than cold reason that will determine much of what they believe. Indeed, it is for this reason that, once a decision has been made, there will be a psychological need to defend the decision, helping to explain why people who disagree can so easily be led to the extremes of their position, where there is no room left for calm discussion.

For those who choose unbelief, the personal experience will almost certainly include suffering, perhaps in someone close to them, for the presence of so much suffering and evil in the world always has been and always will be the strongest argument for the non-existence of God.

Charles Darwin moved from belief to agnosticism during his lifetime, but less because of his ideas concerning natural selection and more because of the death of his ten-year-old daughter in 1851, and his visceral rejection of certain ideas of eternal damnation prevalent at his time.[15]

For my own part, I have often experienced moments of helplessness before the sufferings and tragedies that happen to innocent people, and I would never wish to minimise this particular indication of God's non-existence. Where is God when a baby dies? I shall return to this point.

At the same time, I feel that atheism has been given too easy a passage in recent years. It has too often been allowed to limit itself to criticising and ridiculing the many and glaring defects of the worst kinds of organised religion, especially in its fundamentalist forms. It has been allowed to present itself as science when it is in fact an act of faith that goes beyond the provable evidence.

Most important for me, it does not address the longings within my heart. When atheists appear on television as too superior and rational, they can convey the message that they are as certain of the answers to the major questions of life as the fundamentalists claim to be, and I instinctively feel that we can never have that kind of certainty on either side of this debate. In particular, if they give me no indication that they experience the longings and uncertainties that I feel, they do not speak to my heart.

There is always the option of agnosticism, that is, of saying that one does not know whether God exists or not. If we base ourselves strictly on scientific proof, this may well be the most honest option, but for me it is an unsatisfactory option, for it runs the risk of incurring the worst effects of both sides. It does not answer my longing for love and meaning, while on the other hand, it leaves the problem of suffering untouched.

---

15 See Alister McGrath, *The Twilight of Atheism*, Rider Publications, London, 2004, pp.104-105.

WHAT KIND OF GOD?

Having arrived at this point, I realised that I could not go any further until I had first thought about the kind of god I was being invited to accept or reject, for it is impossible to decide in favour of a false and harmful idea of the divine. Indeed, I believe that the best way for a believer to have a useful discussion with an atheist is to ask, "What kind of god do you not believe in?", for this can lead to large areas of agreement between believers and unbelievers.

A rationalist might say, "First prove that God exists and then you can talk about what kind of God." But it simply doesn't work like that, for I cannot believe in the wrong kind of God. The two questions need to go together.

The dilemma is evident in the debates between reason and faith in the nineteenth century, when a number of religious people made the mistake of trying to answer science on its own terms and offer scientific proofs of their beliefs. In the "Monkey Trial" William Jennings Bryan was doomed to defeat from the first moment he tried to assert that the Bible is not just a book of faith, but also a book of science. In the same way, the people I speak of were doomed to defeat, for there are no scientific proofs of God, and the misguided attempt to provide such proofs has caused two hundred years of difficulties for religion.

In particular, this misguided attempt led to the idea of what has been called "the theistic God" – an elderly white male sitting on a throne as ruler, lawgiver and judge, seeing every single wrong thing done and demanding high standards of conduct. This was the origin of my "God of the high jump" and a-theism arose as the rejection of this theism. It is by far the most common idea of God in the Western world today. If the word "God" is used in the media, it is most probable that this is the idea that both the speaker or writer and the audience have in mind.

I agree wholeheartedly with the rejection of this God, for it is an idol created by human beings rather than a real God. If there is to be the slightest hope of faith, reason and feelings working together, it can never be on the basis of this false and misleading idea of God.

In speaking about the kind of God I might believe in, there are three basic comments that I feel I need to make.

AN "OTHERNESS" BEYOND WORDS AND LANGUAGE

The first comment is that, if a God who created this universe out of nothing exists, he, she or it must be so far above us that not merely can we not imagine God, but we don't even have the language to talk about the subject. Against theism we must say that God is as much female as male, as much black as white, each of the three pronouns "he, she or it" is false, and even the word "exists" implies one being among many and runs the danger of our thinking of a being like ourselves, only bigger. The same is true of any other language we try to use.

> The catechism definition I learned at the age of eight – 'God is the Supreme Spirit, who alone exists of himself and is infinite in all perfections' – was not only dry, abstract and rather boring, but it was also incorrect... I was not taught to ... see that God is not a spirit; that 'he' has no gender; and that we have no idea what we mean when we say that a being 'exists' who is 'infinite in all perfections'. The process that should have led to a stunned appreciation of an 'otherness' beyond the reach of language ended prematurely.[16]

The only language we have to speak about a god who created the universe is that of analogy. To use an analogy means to

---

16 Karen Armstrong, *The Case for God*, The Bodley Head, London, 2009, p.307.

say that something more difficult to describe or understand is "like" something we are more familiar with. But analogies can carry us only so far in our understanding, and in many cases that is not very far. It is said that all analogies limp, and we must add that some crawl, and some don't move at all.

In trying to explain Einstein's General Theory of Relativity to amateurs many scientists have used the same analogy. They tell us to imagine a taut mattress. If we roll a tennis ball along it, it will move in a straight line. But if we place a heavy metal ball on the mattress and then roll the tennis ball, it will move sideways and downwards towards the heavy ball.[17] They then say that the General Theory of Relativity is "like" this. Other scientists will promptly respond and say that this does not begin to explain the theory, it is nothing "like" it. They may, however, be forced to add that they don't have a better analogy.

One of religion's most difficult problems is that, when speaking of God, analogy is the only language we have, and yet absolutely nothing we know in our entire universe is remotely "like" God. So the scientist's problems in speaking about the General Theory of Relativity are as nothing compared to the problems of the religious person in speaking about God.

Scientists who do actually understand the General Theory of Relativity can sometimes be smug in their superiority over those who do not. And unfortunately, in any religion there is always the deep-seated temptation for authorities to do the same, and think that they understand God better than others, that in some manner they "possess" God and can dispense God to others. There is always the temptation to say far more about the infinite God than mere human beings can.

I could not believe in a god whom human beings "possess" or can explain. So I need to remind myself constantly that a true

17 I have borrowed this from Bill Bryson, *A Short History of Nearly Everything*, A Black Swan Book, 2004, p.166.

relationship with any real god involves a never-ending search. And in that search I can never discover "facts" about God in the way a scientist can discover facts about nature.

As a result, my constant search for truth is more important than the few shreds of truth I might possess. My constant and genuine search to find moral goodness is more important than any particular moral truths I have come to. My search for answers to questions of evil and suffering is more important than any answers I think I might have found. And my search for God is far more important than the pathetically weak human ideas of God that are present in my mind and imagination.

Sacred writings are a search, morality is a search, the spiritual life is a search, life itself is a search, love is a search and God is a search. There will never be a time in this life when I can stop searching because I am in possession of all that I need to find. I can never "possess" God in my tiny mind, and it is far healthier to think in terms of a god who constantly surprises me by being different from any preconceived ideas I have had.

I must never forget the necessity for a profound humility. I know that when I stand up in church to give a homily, no matter how confident I may appear, the thought is always with me, "What am I doing up here? What do I have to say to the real lives of these people in front of me?"

ANGRY AND LOVING GODS

The second comment I need to make about the kind of god I might believe in comes from the fears and longings within every human being.

I have recently read the book *Infidel*, the moving autobiography of Ayaan Hirsi Ali.[18] She was born in Somalia and subjected to all the restrictions placed on a young female

18 Pocket Books, Simon and Schuster, London, 2007.

under Islamic law in a poor and harsh country. At age five she was, without anaesthetic, genitally excised on the kitchen table of her home. In her young life there was always an abundance of males telling her what she must do, and the high jumps imposed on her were far more restrictive than anything ever presented to me. Eventually she was married against her will to a man from Canada, but on her way there she passed through Europe and escaped to live in The Netherlands. There she eventually rejected her religion and became an atheist.

If personal experience and what one wants to believe are the most important factors in deciding between belief and unbelief, then I fully understand why she chose unbelief. Whatever beautiful words about God might have been quoted to her, in fact and in practice her early life had been governed by an horrendously strict and demanding god, and she absolutely had to reject this false god before she could move forward in her life. I realise that, if my early life had been in any way similar to hers, I, too, might well be an atheist today.

This is where our fears become important, for our longings can lead us to the idea of the divine, but our fears then lead us astray to the idea of an angry god. The many powerful male figures who spoke to Ayaan Hirsi Ali of God certainly spoke of an angry God and attempted to use religion to coerce her conduct.

It is unfortunately true that religious authorities in any religion can be so convinced they are right, and hence so determined to impose their ideas on others, that they can use these fears within people to control the conduct and even the thinking of the members of that religion through a stress on a god of anger and control. The "theistic god" fitted into this model.

Whenever this happens, that religion presents a god that a true spirituality cannot respond to. It creates an atmosphere where control of energy is more important than access to and release of creative energy, so that people can not grow to become all they are capable of being. A god of anger represents a religion based on fear rather than love, and so can not answer the longings that led people to the divine in the first place. It induces a negative religion based on blind obedience, self-abasement and rejection of the 'world', rather than a positive seeking of all that is good.

The angry god has been the major contribution of religious belief to the rise of unbelief, for in any religion everything without exception depends on the kind of god who is being worshipped. For any community or individual the first and most important religious question to ask is always: What kind of God is being worshipped here?

More than any other single factor, it is also the worship of an angry god that has been the cause of spirituality and religion being so divided today. If spirituality and religion are to be brought together again, religion must offer a sincere apology for the angry god of the past and show clearly that it has now changed radically and will no longer seek to present an angry god, or use the idea of an angry god to control people.

The change must not be merely words, but must transform all aspects of the religious community, especially all facets of how authority is exercised. People will be utterly unconvinced by claims that there is no need for change, and they will need much convincing that such a profound change has genuinely taken place.

In our own day we have seen a powerful reaction against the angry god, with many people like Ayaan Hirsi Ali simply rejecting that god and moving towards some form of agnosticism or even atheism. Other people, however, whose experience was not as bad as hers, have sensed that the problem has not been the divine itself, but the manner in which the divine has been presented by human beings. Rather than become atheists, they have looked for a sounder understanding of the divine.

Unfortunately, many people have solved the problem of the angry god merely by going to an opposite extreme of a god of soft love. If I may use an analogy with parents (yes, I am using a weak human analogy in an attempt to say something about God), this movement has gone all the way from parents who beat their child into submission to parents who spoil their child. It has created the idea of a god of soft and indulgent love, a god so "loving" that nothing is asked of people and they are challenged to nothing.

Under such a god it is just as certain that people will not grow as it is that spoiled children will not grow as they should. The followers of this god can go so far as to deny the very existence of right and wrong, personal responsibility or standards of conduct. While I fully share the need to reject the angry god, this idea of a god of soft love would also fail to speak to my longings.

My own journey away from the god of the high jump tells me that sound ideas concerning the divine are to be found in the middle ground, between these two extremes. Once again I have no choice but to use a human analogy, with all its weaknesses, and the analogy I choose is that of the good teacher.

If I look back to the best teachers I ever had, I shall always remember them as people who cared about me and wanted the best for me, but loved me with an intelligent love that knew when to praise or console me, and when to challenge me to further effort. Their overriding desire in all they did was that I should grow to become all I was capable of being. In their classrooms there was a place for obedience, but it was never an end in itself. Obedience was only a means, and growth was the end it had to serve. Rather than set up high jumps and demand that I clear the bar, they drew on the desires and longings within me as they sought to inspire me and make me want to grow.

The best of them had a passion for the subject they were teaching and they succeeded in arousing some of that passion within me, so that I wanted to learn more without anyone having to order me to do so. In doing this they constantly placed before me challenges that were appropriate to my age and level of development, for it was in large part by meeting these challenges that I grew. They stand out in my memory, and I shall always be grateful that I had these examples of what good teaching can be.

In a similar way, my journey has led me to the conclusion that the only god I could believe in is a god who wants growth first, and obedience as no more than a means to this end. I know that I could not grow under an angry god and I would not grow under a god of soft, indulgent love. I would have a true freedom to grow only under a god who, like these teachers, loved me and, because of this love, wanted me to grow to become all I was capable of being, and so would not be afraid to challenge me to grow.

DIVINE LOVE AND HUMAN LOVE

There is a third comment I feel I must make on the kind of god I am invited to believe in. In addition to presenting an angry god, religious bodies have all too frequently made a second mistake. I have already mentioned that they can see love as a straight line moving upwards from desire and affection to the higher plane of self-giving and stopping there, rather than as a circle in which self-giving is constantly renewed and replenished by desire and affection.

In doing this, they have spoken of the importance of our love for others, but not of our need to receive love from others and of a proper love of self. There is a simple truth here, but one that I have learned the hard way.

There is today a wealth of material telling me that, while saying "no" to certain desires is often necessary, it is also essential that I say "yes" to my most important needs. In doing this, both the receiving of love from others, and a basic self-love and self-esteem are essential to my freedom to grow. It has been pointed out that being self-centred is far more often the result of self-hating than of self-liking. The self-hating person feels an emptiness within and must fill this void by constantly thinking about self, while the self-liking person can forget self and go out to help others.[19]

It is also true that all love should benefit two people, the lover and the one loved.[20] I can deny myself any unnecessary material goods, I can deny my comfort, advantage or convenience, but in loving others I should not deny my own deepest good or spiritual growth. I must absolutely receive love as well as give it, and my love for others must be a love that gives both them and myself the freedom to grow.

> (We) cannot live by oblative, descending love alone. (We) cannot always give, (we) must also receive. Anyone who wishes to give love must also receive love as a gift.[21]

To have this freedom to grow, I must learn to combine self-denial with self-love. During the Olympic Games in Beijing I watched on television the best athletes in the world striving for that something "faster, higher and stronger". I knew that for each of them there had been a vast amount of grinding hard work and pain, and, therefore, of self-denial and renunciation,

19 Cf. John Powell, *Happiness is an Inside Job,* Tabor Publishing, Valencia, California, 1989, p.14.
20 cf. M Scott Peck, *The Road Less Travelled,* Arrow Books, London, 1990, pp.118-123.
21 Pope Benedict XVI, *op.cit.,* no.7.

before they qualified for these Games. At the same time, it was obvious that most of them had abundant self-belief, self-esteem and self-confidence (think of Usain Bolt!), or they would never have had the courage to begin the long journey to this moment, let alone complete it.[22]

Those who believe in God also need to combine the greatest degree of self-giving and hard work for others with the conviction that they can actually make a difference and do the things that their God most wants for this world.

When Mahatma Gandhi began his campaign of non-violent disobedience, he had to believe that he could be an instrument in causing even the might of the British Empire to fall. When Martin Luther King Jr. began to march, he had to believe that these marches could overcome deep and bitter prejudice and bring civil rights to his people. When Nelson Mandela came out of prison talking of reconciliation and of all races in South Africa working together, he had to believe that the walls of apartheid could come down. And when Mother Teresa left her convent, she had to believe that, with the help of her God, she could make a difference to the lives of some of the poorest in Calcutta. And in all cases, whether these people actually made a difference is less important than that they made every effort to do so.

I feel now that the church of my early years gave me mixed

---

22 The word "ascetic" is derived from the Greek word *askesis,* meaning "practice". In this original sense the athlete was always an ascetic, one who practised constantly. Deriving from this, "ascetic" came to mean that the virtuous person constantly practised virtue. It was only later that the word acquired the negative meaning of self-punishment for sinfulness and involved a separation of mind and body, such that "I" punished my "body". There has more recently been a return to the original meaning, though the word itself remains contaminated by the negative meanings. See the entry on Asceticism in *The New Dictionary of Catholic Spirituality,*The Liturgical Press, Collegeville, pp.63-65.

messages on these subjects. While it certainly tried to inspire me to aim high, I feel that it failed me to the extent that it presented an opposition between love of God and a proper love of the world around me, or when it told me to turn my back on "the world" and be concerned exclusively with "the spirit", or when it spoke continually of self-denial but without speaking of self-love, or stressed the need to love but not the need to be loved, or praised *agape* but tended to diminish *philia* and despise *eros*, or spoke of belief in God but downplayed the need for belief in self. Dealing with these conflicting messages implanted within me in my early years has had to be a large part of my spiritual journey.

THE HEART LEADING THE HEAD

Once I had arrived at this basic level of understanding of the kind of God I was being invited to believe in, I had to face the question of belief or unbelief. In the situation in which I found myself, I tried hard to put aside any public position I had held and to ask myself as honestly as I could, "When everything else has been put aside, what do I really believe in the depths of my own mind and heart?"

In trying to answer this question, I came to realise that the major change within myself was that my reasoning was now based far more on the desires within me rather than on rational arguments drawn from facts outside myself. I can at least express some of the elements:

— The desires within me are so powerful and so constant that they control every thought and action of my life. Do they come from God or are they the result of chemical or physical forces within me?

— Is it possible to find a satisfying sense of meaning in this world without God?

—In this world there is both evil and suffering on the one
hand, and a marvellous beauty and grandeur on the other.
I will always remain deeply troubled by the suffering,
but in balancing the suffering and the beauty, am I still
glad I was born or do I want to reject this world?

—Since the time of Aristotle we have known that many
ethical principles can be stated without the need for any
reference to God. Are these principles sufficient, or do
I still feel that to exclude God would leave me without
an adequate and satisfying basis in deciding where true
goodness lies and how I might move towards it?

—Without being able to fully explain why, I believe
passionately in the equal human dignity of all people.
If God is excluded, can I find an adequate basis for that
dignity?

—In the bush I am lost if I have no point of reference beyond
myself. In life itself would I be lost if I had no point of
reference beyond myself?

—Do I find reflections, however pale, of something higher
in every person I meet? Do they somehow point beyond
themselves to greater beauty, truth and goodness, or is
this just self-deception?

—On occasions I have met what I believed were moments
of genuine holiness in others. Was it real and where did
it come from?

—While I hope that I love science and all the good things it
has produced, do I also need myth, story and symbol in
order to live a satisfying life?

—Was the Big Bang an explosion of God's love or did it
happen without any intelligent cause?

—I have never met or heard of any person remotely as
inspiring as Jesus Christ and he remains a constant
beacon for my life. Did he not merely believe in God

but, in his words and actions and very person, bring the divine to earth? In him do I finally meet that divine love I have longed for?

I freely acknowledge that none of these factors can give any final <u>proof</u> of the existence of God. And yet they do express a significant part of my own personal journey, and indicate the matters I have been thinking about.

A WORLD OF EVIL AND SUFFERING

Of all the questions just raised, the one that most troubles me is that of the sheer weight of evil and suffering in the world. My starting point is that those who feel no contradiction between a god of love and the fact of overwhelming human suffering, and those who reject God altogether, have in common that they both believe that they have found the answer and so have ceased to search. And yet evil and suffering are a reality so deep that I am convinced that this kind of certainty cannot exist on either side.

If, however, it is not possible to give "answers" to questions concerning evil and suffering in the world, is it at least possible to give food for thought?

All attempts to explain suffering must speak directly to the victims, and not be simply a defence of our own ideas about the divine. We must start by freely admitting that the suffering of many people is so terrible that believers in God can be reduced to feelings of helpless impotence, and many victims have every right to rage at the unfairness of their suffering.

Yes, those who smoke or eat too much are at greater risk of heart attack and we should not blame God for that. But there is so much quite undeserved suffering in the world, and the jarring conflict between this and a God of love is so radical that suffering must continue to cry out and irritate our thoughts.

There is not, and cannot be, any positive meaning in the kind of unjust and terrible suffering that destroys persons, and we must refuse to justify, ignore, spiritualise or glorify it. Instead, we need to cry out, protest, lament and shout indignation at the injustice of much suffering

If we believe in God, it must be a god who actually welcomes this rage. It must be a god who sees rage as a positive first response, a denial that all suffering is based on justice, and hence a necessary and proper affirmation of self. A false modern piety has disapproved of this rage, but the Bible is full of it (e.g. Job and the Psalms), and even Jesus cried out at God's seeming abandonment of him.

We should never say that God does not cause suffering, but only allows it, for a god who created a world containing cancer is responsible for the suffering of cancer; a god who could prevent a tsunami or earthquake or cot death, and does not do so, is responsible for the suffering caused.

We should never use false platitudes: "Suffering is a punishment for sin", "In the end good will triumph", "God has good reasons for all that happens", "Parents often make their children do unwanted things", "Suffering is sent as a test to strengthen us", "It is God's will". Such statements might make the speaker feel better, but they do nothing for the person suffering.

On the other hand, even in the lowest forms of life there is an inherent struggle towards something higher and better, an insistent thrusting upwards and forwards. The whole of creation shares in this vital life principle of the striving for growth.

May the Big Bang itself be seen as an explosion of God's love, with the whole universe meant to grow, both in quantity and in quality, until it in some manner returns to God's love? May everything in the universe, and everything in the life of individuals and the human race itself, be seen in terms of this growth? May the entire purpose of the world be summed up in that one word: Growth?

If God exists, then it is clearly intended that we should live in a world of randomness, uncertainty and suffering. It seems to be also clearly intended that we should bring to this random world all the order and certainty we can and overcome all the suffering we can. This seems to be an essential element of our growth.

While I have grown through the tasks that I set myself, much of my most important growing has come from my response to the things that happened to me from outside, that I did not want or welcome and that somehow took me down to the depths of my being. In other words, the very randomness of suffering has made its own contribution to my growth.

Attending to material satisfactions in a consumer society, people can think that anything painful needs to be expelled. When suffering does arrive at their doorstep, they do not know how to achieve meaning. They can, therefore, insulate themselves in banal activities instead of risking a life of engagement.

And yet, our most profound experiences tell us that life is not an intellectual problem to be solved, but a mystery to be lived. There is no statement that will "explain" human life, and it is only by living it at its depths, and opening ourselves to the full pain and tragedy of the world, that we grow to a deeper understanding.

There are powerful desires within each of us, some more superficial, some more profound. It is only when we put aside the more superficial, and seek to respond to the most profound desires in the very depths of our being, that we come to a deeper understanding of our own lives. There are no shortcuts to this understanding.

There is a medical condition in which the nerves do not transmit sensations to the brain, and persons with this condition feel no physical pain. This might seem highly desirable until we remember that they also feel no physical pleasure, and receive no warnings of problems arising in the body. We must think very carefully indeed before we decide that a world without any suffering would be ideal.

Free will, the freedom to choose between right and wrong, is our greatest possession, at the very heart of our ability to grow as human beings. Unless we had the freedom to choose what is wrong and harmful, we could not choose what is good and helpful. The only way the harmful effects of wrong choices could be prevented would be by the taking away of freewill itself and our consequent ability to grow. If God exists, it seems that God has total respect for human freewill.

When suffering comes into a person's life, there is no basis on which to conclude that this means that God is punishing that person, that God has specially chosen this suffering for this individual. It means only that this is a world in which random suffering occurs. It is pure chance if a rock falls and one person is killed, while another a metre away is unharmed.

When suffering comes, there is frequently no real answer to the question "Why?", and the only question that matters is, "How shall I respond?"

All the people I most esteem suffered greatly as they struggled to be true to themselves, and grew to become people I can admire and imitate. I cannot think of any exceptions to this.

From our perspective this is the only life we know, and yet, if God exists, there is also eternal life, our individual return to divine love. Eternal life may never be used as an excuse for not doing everything we possibly can to overcome the suffering in this world, but, if it exists, it is an overwhelming fact that would change the very way we see this world.

For a person who believes in the Christian religion the only response God has ever given to the problems created by the existence of suffering has been, not to take it away, but in Jesus to share it with us. Jesus died, not because of some divine will, nor to fulfil a saying in Scripture, nor to placate an angry god, but because he had to be true to himself in the face of human demands that he conform to lesser ideas. Though he possessed power, he had to show the superiority of the ways of love, whatever the cost.

Where was God at Auschwitz? Auschwitz proves that God will never take away human freewill, not even when it chooses to do the most terrible things, for to take away freewill would be to destroy growth. The best we can say is that God was present in the minds and hearts of those suffering, crying out to the world through them at the inhumanity of all such actions.

I am well aware that every single statement just made leads to more questions than answers, but so does the total denial of God. Our deepest convictions need to be that we must never cease to search, and that living this world's pain and working to diminish it is more important than any intellectual thinking about it.

Perhaps there is wisdom in the seemingly unscientific logic of the Buddhist nun, Pema Chodron,

> Instead of transcending the suffering of all creatures, we move towards the turbulence and doubt. We tiptoe into it. We move toward it however we can. We explore the reality and unpredictability of insecurity and pain, and we try not to push it away. If it takes years, if it takes lifetimes, we let it be as it is. At our own pace, without speed or aggression, we move down and down and down. With us move millions of others, our companions in awakening from fear. Right down there, in the thick of things we discover the love that will not die.[23]

---

23 *When Things Fall Apart: heart advice for difficult times,* quoted in *The Tablet,* 21 March 2009, p.25.

IMMERSING MYSELF

Needless to say, it would not be enough to come to intellectual belief in the existence of God. In line with everything I have said so far, I must, before I come to a decision, think about what that belief might mean to me, that is, what kind of relationship I would want to have with this God.

In thinking about this question, I realised that, since it was the desires within me that had led me to this point, it surely followed that there would be no sense in adopting a form of relationship with God that would not and could not speak to those desires. This grew large in my thinking for, as I looked around, I felt that extraordinarily large numbers of people do precisely this. Indeed, it is one of the largest problems connected with religious belief.

Some can say, in effect: "I have finally decided on belief rather than unbelief, but it was a close battle, and I am less than certain. I still have massive problems with the defects I see in many religious bodies. So I am dipping my toe in the sea of religious belief, but I am definitely not diving in. I shall rather watch each element closely and decide on exactly which parts I will accept and which parts I will not. I shall never in any way surrender to God, for at all times I must be firmly in charge of the relationship."

Others can say: "I am still afraid that there might be angry aspects to God. So just to be sure, I shall do all I have to do to placate an angry god, and my major concern will be, not so much to speak to the deepest longings within my heart, but to solve all my problems by getting into heaven in the next life."

Yet others can, in effect, be saying: "Lord, let's make a commercial contract. I will believe all of the truths you have revealed, I will do my best to obey the moral rules you have decreed, I will go to church every Sunday, and I will be a paid up member of the church, and you in return will give me eternal life, (oh, and by the way, you'll make things easier for me in this life too)."

None of these attitudes could or would speak to the deepest longings within me. They would inevitably leave me dissatisfied, for the truths of religion would be lifeless, the moral rules would be burdensome tasks and the worship would be empty. I believe that attitudes such as these are the major reason why so many people accept religious belief, but then find little satisfaction in it, and live it at a superficial level. They are also one of the major reasons why so many people reject the religion that they see around them, for the type of religion I have just described is hardly attractive.

In deciding between belief and unbelief I felt that I needed to say to myself, "There are no scientific proofs either way, only indications, so this is one of the most difficult but also most important decisions I shall ever make. And yet I must make a decision, for to sit forever on the fence between the two is no answer. So, despite all my reservations, I must either dive fully into the sea of belief, or dive fully into the sea of unbelief. This makes the choice even more difficult, but there is no alternative. It was my longing for love that led me here, so if I dive into the sea of belief, it is to a love relationship that I must abandon myself, for nothing less would really speak to my longings."

In trying to base myself firmly on the powerful desires within me, I found this thought overwhelming: Religion makes sense only as a love relationship. Anything less than this will not bring real satisfaction and will, indeed, cause much frustration and disappointment. Anything less than a love relationship will never win the battle for the imagination of people, or tempt them beyond their individualism.

Yes, there are profound fears in the idea of a love relationship with God, for I do not know what such a relationship might ask of me. I am afraid that it will inevitably draw me to enter more deeply into myself, and to rise closer to becoming all that I am capable of being. These are profound thoughts and they cause profound fears.

It would be easy to hold back from such a commitment and seek to be in control of my religious beliefs. I could then accept God but make sure I kept God at a certain distance. I could even use the formal prayers of religion as a way of being polite to God and saying all the right things, but without actually having to say and mean anything as frightening as "I love you".

And yet the holding back, the less than total commitment, would inevitably harm my personal relationship with God, the obligations of belief would immediately begin to become burdensome and the relationship would no longer speak to the needs that brought me to it in the first place.

A CERTAINTY, TWO CONVICTIONS AND A STEP OF FAITH

In thinking about these matters I have finally found that within me there is a certainty, two convictions and a step of faith.

The certainty is that everything within me instinctively and strongly recoils from the idea of diving fully into the sea of unbelief and entrusting my whole life to it. If there are no proofs of the existence of God, there are equally no proofs of the non-existence of God, so it would not be an easier act of faith than belief in God. And the world of unbelief does not speak to the longings that are now at the centre of my thinking and feeling, so there is little to entice me to dive into that sea. The only enticement might be a feeling of freedom and autonomy from the constraints of religion, but I find that this is nowhere near as powerful as my longing for love. I could not ever be a convinced and serene atheist. I don't belong there and I could not base my life on it. For me this is a certainty.

The first conviction is that I could not sit forever on the fence between belief and unbelief. I could not live my whole life there, for it would leave all of my deepest desires unanswered.

The second conviction is one I have already stated, that is, that I will not reject my past unless I can replace it with something truly satisfying, and I could never use the adjective "satisfying" of unbelief.

The step of faith is that my firm starting point was "love's urgent longings", and belief in God is by far the best answer I can find to those longings. I lack proofs and I will forever have problems about the evil and suffering that fill this world, and yet the indications of God's existence speak to me, above all in the person and story of Jesus Christ. They speak to me to the extent that, despite all difficulties, I am prepared to dive into the sea of belief and accept the consequence that this must involve a love relationship.

This is a step of faith, not a scientific or philosophical certainty, so it was not a graceful dive that I took. But here I am in the water.

A LOVE RELATIONSHIP

I cannot imagine God and I do not even have the language to talk about God. So how can I have a love relationship with someone who is so absent, whom I cannot imagine, see or hear, let alone reach out to and touch, and who never seems to answer when I speak? How can I take the example of any form of love relationship I have ever experienced and apply it to God?

The answer I have finally come to is that, while love can involve powerful feelings, true love resides in the will as well as in the feelings, for it always includes two desires. If I think of all the most important loves of my life, I know that in each case I wanted two things: I wanted that person to be an important part of my life, and I wanted all that was good for that person. In most cases I wanted those two things so much that my feelings were spontaneously involved and I felt deep within me the strong desires, needs and yearnings that we think of when we speak of love.

I have said "in most cases", for there can be circumstances in which the desires and the feelings do not go together. I remember the mother of an adult son saying to me, "Most of the time I can't stand him, but I still love him", and we all know what she meant. After constant and serious disappointments over many years she had become so exasperated and angry with her son that most of her instinctive feelings were negative rather than positive, and yet her love itself remained unconditional. She knew that there would never be a time when she stopped wanting him to be part of her life and there would never be a time when she did not want all that was good for him. While it is always good that the feelings and the desires should go together, the feelings can sometimes be absent, and yet love remains because the two desires remain.

When the Hebrew scriptures tell me to love my neighbour as I love myself[24], they do not mean that I must have warm feelings for my neighbour. They mean that my relationships with the people around me should be an important part of my life, and that I should do all I can to promote their good, especially those who are in need. In other words, they mean that I should constantly have, and act on, the two desires.[25]

---

24 Leviticus 19:18

25 There is also, of course, the Christian injunction to "love your enemies" (Mt.5:44). How can one love someone like Adolf Hitler or Pol Pot or Sadam Hussein? We can still want all that is good for them, understanding that this will involve very serious change in every aspect of their lives. The sense in which we might want our enemies collectively to be an important part of our lives would need much further consideration, and that is beyond the scope of this book.

In my relationship with God, feelings of love often seem to be absent, and I could conclude that love is, therefore, not present. But the two desires can be present, whether the feelings are present or not, so I must now look at those two desires.

AN IMPORTANT PART OF MY LIFE

It was the profound desire for love that led me to God, so I want God to be part of everything in my life: my family, my work, my recreation and all my relationships.

From other relationships in my life I know that, when I want someone to be an important part of my life, it is probable that the single most important element is that the two of us begin to listen to each other's story. This story will include many external details, but it will also gradually include the story of feelings, hopes, fears, yearnings and needs. It will include the story of the many ways in which the deep longings within us manifest themselves. It will gradually include memories of childhood events that were significant in the fulfilling or frustrating of these longings. Developing a love relationship with God will inevitably involve the same sharing of stories, as I learn more about God and share more of my own story with God.

I can easily think that the infinite God already knows my story, so I don't need to tell it. But even if I don't need to tell it for God's sake, I do for my own sake. I have only gradually understood where my story has been leading me, and often it was in telling the story to others that I gained insight into it. God can be my audience as I struggle to understand.

Concerning God's story, I have needed to remind myself that countless people have struggled with the search for God before me, and I would be foolish if I was not willing to learn from them. Just as I cannot sit forever on the fence between belief and unbelief and carefully evaluate every single element before committing myself to anything, so I cannot make a careful study of every single element of every single attempt to understand God in order to form my own synthesis.

In the real world I need to enter into one of the religious traditions that people have formed. Only in this way can I really hope to know something of God's story and see God as a real person I can relate to. Which tradition to enter into is, of course, a major decision, but it is a decision that must be made.

Any religious tradition comes to me covered with a million additions placed there by human beings, obscuring and distorting it. Unfortunately it is impossible to avoid this reality. And yet it is the essential story behind all the human additions that needs to be the true focus of my attention, for I must do my best to separate the story of God from the many human misunderstandings of God. So my need is both to enter into a religious tradition and to think as intelligently as I can about that tradition. I shall return to this concept of story.

Loving What God Loves

The second essential desire of love is to desire all that is good for the one loved. And to desire all that is good for God means, I believe, to desire with all my being what God desires. If I love another person, I will want to see all the deepest desires of that person's life fulfilled. And if I love God, I will want to see all of God's deepest desires for this world fulfilled.

And that will always bring me back immediately to the twin commandments of the Hebrew scriptures: to love God with all my heart and soul and strength and mind, and to love my neighbour as myself. That the two commandments must go together, that I cannot love God unless I love the people around me, is both a theological and a psychological truth.

This will mean that I cannot just want to "get into heaven", but must be totally involved in the needs of people here and now in this world, seeking to build a better world. If my sole or major desire were the selfish one of "getting into heaven", it is certain that I would fall into some form of commercial relationship with God rather than one of love. If spirituality is not related to justice and love for others, it is self-serving.

I believe that God gave this world into the hands of human beings and then stepped back to let them take responsibility, make their mistakes and, by this process, gradually become all they are capable of being. In other words, I believe that God treats us as adults, not as children.

I believe it is God's intention that the harm caused by malaria or cancer or HIV-AIDS should be overcome, but by human endeavour rather than by a divine miracle, for it is only through this endeavour that human beings will grow. I believe that God hates the poverty, starvation and misery of so many people on this planet, but has no intention of curing it by some great miracle, for it is meant to be a work of human beings.

I believe that growth, both of individuals and of the whole human race, is the very purpose of this world, the deepest desire of God. If I want what God wants, then I, too, will want this growth. So to want a love relationship with God that will answer the depth of the longing for love within my heart means to commit myself both to becoming all I am capable of being and to doing all I can to help the world to grow.

Having said all of this, I also believe that God loved me long before I loved God, and that God works within me and through me. So I do not seek to do all of this work alone, without God. I rather see the work and the love relationship as supporting each other and growing together.

It is in this dual task of constantly returning to the love relationship with God and constantly seeking to reach out to others that I come closest to finding the infinite love I crave.

Having arrived at this point, the next step is to see how I can best make God an important part of my life by entering into one of the religious traditions around me and, at the same time, make this world a better place by working with others.

3

LONGING FOR COMMUNITY

The striving to respond to my desire for infinite love has led me to belief in God, so God is now an essential part of my spirituality, my seeking of higher goals. Everything I said about desires in the first chapter now needs to be seen in this light. And reaching out to God essentially involves reaching out to other people, so my relationship with other people is also an integral part of my spirituality.

Indeed, I feel the need for two complementary forms of reaching out. I want to reach out to all those God loves, especially those most in need of love. And, because on my own I cannot begin to meet the needs of all people, I feel a spontaneous need to reach out to other people so that together we may more effectively reach out to those in need.

In the language of integrated energy, my desire to reach out to the neediest requires the fire that comes from God, while my need to work together with other people requires the water of control of my personal wishes so that I might more effectively work as part of a team.

This raises the problem of where I might find a group or community of people who would share powerful and satisfying ideals with me, such that I could work with God and with them in reaching out to others.

THE BEAUTY OF THE STORY

At the heart of every community and every nation there is a story, and the members of the community or nation find strength and meaning in that story. For example, France has a story, Russia has a story, China has a story, and that story is essential to what it means to be French or Russian or Chinese.

The same is true of religious bodies. In Judaism its foundation is in the story of Moses, the escape from slavery in Egypt and the coming into the Promised Land. For Christians it is the same story, but then built on it is the story of the life and death and resurrection of Jesus. For Muslims it is the story of how Mohammed brought a whole people to belief in one God in a few years and gave them a profound sense of identity. This story then becomes a major means by which the members of a particular religion gain access to their experience of God's love.

I have lived all my life within the religious tradition of the story of Jesus Christ. I still find that story so satisfying that I would never wish to abandon it. I recognise that other religious traditions have their unique insights into the divine, and I hope I can learn from them, but I have no desire to replace the Christian story with any other.

Jesus Christ remains the single most admirable and inspiring person I have known or heard of, and any problems I have experienced in recent years are not to be found in him. Through his story I have gained much of my own personal experience of divine love, and the story constantly renews me. It will always be within the Christian world that I first seek the community I can belong to and work with, for that will always be the place where I find the greatest inspiration.

My religious faith is first and foremost faith in the person and story of Jesus Christ. From that story flow a series of truths that I believe, moral rules that I seek to follow, worship that I willingly give, and a religious community of people to which I have belonged, but the response to the person and story comes first.

Without a love relationship with the person at the heart of the story, the truths would become lifeless, the norms of living would be burdensome tasks, the worship would be empty, and the community would be in danger of becoming a soulless institution. I would be back to knowing a lot about Jesus but never having actually met him.

With the relationship, the truths come alive, the norms of living are the most natural things in the world, the worship is life-giving, and the community is a source of strength and support. If the love relationship is taken out of religion, all that is left is nothing more than empty formalism.

It is in that person and story, more than anywhere else, that I most powerfully feel that God is constantly saying to me, "I love you". And I feel that it can never be enough to answer, "I believe all the truths you have revealed" or "I will obey all of your commands" or "I will go to church every Sunday" or "I will be a paid up member of the church". The only genuine answer is a response of love to love, and that means a response of my whole person – my mind, my heart, my feelings and my very core.

Truths, norms of living, worship and community all have their legitimate and important place, but religious faith must never be reduced to intellectual assent to truths, external compliance with norms of living, physical attendance at public worship or membership of an institution. Presenting faith as a series of propositions and moral rules to be learned by heart can never be a substitute for the passing on of a living faith in a person and a story.

At every moment of every day God is saying to me through this story, "I love you. There are no conditions. I love you exactly as you are, with all your faults and weaknesses. I do not demand that you change into a better person before I will begin to love you." This and nothing else is the foundation of my religious faith, and that faith is born when I can begin to answer, however timidly, "I love you too".

I am determined, therefore, to remain within the Christian story and find in it my inspiration to work for others.

A problem arises, however, from the fact that there is such a close link between the basic story and the practical beliefs, moral rules, worship and community that flow from it. The problem is that there is inevitably so much human input into the beliefs, rules, worship and community that the beautiful basic story can become obscured and contaminated. If I could somehow abstract the basic story out of all the human messiness that surrounds it it, I would be happy. But this is not possible and my only choice is either to abandon the basic story or to live that story in the middle of a human community.

This forces on me the question of whether the particular Christian church I have belonged to all my life is still a good place for me to develop a love relationship with God and reach out to others?

A COMMUNITY OF HUMAN BEINGS

All communities share the same profound flaw that they are made up of ordinary human beings. And the higher the ideals they put before themselves, the more obvious these flaws will be. In a particular way, every religious community faces the impossible problem that it seeks to deal with the deepest, most beautiful and most subtle of human desires, but is made up of human beings with all their fears and longings, their greatness and pettiness, and the struggle between good and evil that is always present within their hearts.

It is impossible to put two human beings together, no matter how noble the purpose, without also introducing competition, politics and the fight between love of neighbour and love of self. There never has been a perfect religious community and there never will be. I must always take this as my starting point.

And yet there have been many times in recent years when I found this a hard truth to accept. I was used to squabbling and disputes in the church, I was used to inflated egos and I was used to people being intransigent in their views, and I could cope with all of that, for I knew that I was no better than others.

But then, when the revelations of sexual abuse began to appear, I was overwhelmed by just how far short too many people fell of the ideals they proclaimed, and this on a matter that concerned the safety of innocent children, and so pierced to the very heart of the church.

I was heartened when I saw genuine change and development in many individuals, but I felt despair when I saw that the institution itself was not willing to change in any of its central structures and attitudes, and was refusing even to look at whether any of its teachings concerning power or sex might need to be revisited. The teachings and even the laws were set in stone and could not be looked at again, *not even if they were contributing to abuse.* In too many people there was also an attitude of fear and protectiveness of the institution of the church that was simply not Christian. The Christian response to such a crisis is courage, not fear; openness, not protectiveness.

As a minor I had been a victim of sexual abuse myself and I cannot really put into words how profoundly I was disillusioned by what happened within the Catholic Church in those years. I went through a very bad period and, even while still working as a bishop, seriously wondered whether there was any place for me in the church. It is no accident that I retired as a bishop soon after my official work in this field came to an end.

During those years I was assisted and, indeed, inspired by many of the victims themselves, and I shall always owe them a great debt of gratitude. I was also helped by the many Catholic people who worked hard to reach out to victims.

But I have to add that, paradoxically, what most helped me to survive that period was the realisation that I was myself a senior official of the church, so I could not take the easy way out of simply separating myself from what was happening. Though I was constantly tempted to an "us" and "them" attitude, I had to keep reminding myself that, like it or not, I was also one of "them".

It is impossible to satisfy all the needs of victims of abuse, for it is impossible to undo the past and take away the damage, and I had to admit that there had been occasions when victims had seen me as failing them, so the ugly face of the church they believed they saw had been my own face. If I did not recognise this, I would be making myself superior to others, and that was the very attitude that had led to much of the abuse and to the worst aspects of the response to abuse.

This helped me to understand that, if I turn away in disgust from every place where I believe I see hypocrisy, I will soon run out of communities and have nowhere else to go. And I will probably not be able to look at myself in the mirror either.

The only way to avoid hypocrisy would be not to make any claims of striving towards higher goals, but it would be a great pity if I or anyone else took that path.

Without ever ceasing to demand that religious communities constantly reform themselves and come closer to the ideals they proclaim, I must accept that no human community can escape its humanity. No community that looks to the divine can ever afford to forget that it is itself human.

THE UGLY AND THE BEAUTIFUL

At a time when he was struggling with the idea of whether to join the Catholic Church, John Henry Newman wrote in a letter to a friend, "There is nothing on this earth so ugly as the

Catholic Church, and nothing so beautiful." The same could probably be said of any religious body, though I recognise that Newman was saying that in his eyes both ugliness and beauty seemed to be taken to their extreme in the Catholic Church, and in this I must agree with him.

The Catholic Church is one of the largest and oldest institutions on earth, and has had ample time to acquire an immense history of ugliness. Unworthy popes, crusades, inquisitions, buying and selling the spiritual, siding with the strong against the weak, the use of fear to coerce people, ambition, an inflated authority stifling initiative, and the sexual abuse of minors are among many things that go to create this vast, overwhelming history of ugliness, an ugliness so great that it threatens to crush anyone who ventures near it and can stunt the life of anyone who seeks to live within it.

To those who know it well, however, there is also great beauty in the Catholic Church. I have found it in some church leaders, such as Pope John XXIII (1958-63), the martyr bishop Oscar Romero (killed in 1980 in El Salvador because he had become the voice of the weak against the powerful), and countless others less famous but no less inspiring.

I have seen it in dedicated, harassed and overworked fellow priests trying to meet the varied and conflicting demands of a whole parish. I have seen it in the commitment and love of religious nuns and brothers who have reached out to the neediest in so many ways, for Mother Teresa was far from being unique.

And I have seen it in the lives of ordinary Catholic people and in the ordinary events of daily life. I have experienced a profound beauty in the faith-inspired struggle of people to respond to the call they feel to rise above themselves and in their passionate desire to make this world a better place.

I see beauty in the Easter ceremony when a candle

symbolising the risen Christ is the only light in the darkened church, and each person present lights a candle from this one until the darkness of the night is dispelled. I find beauty in a ceremony of baptism or confirmation or ordination.

All my life I have found beauty in the Mass. I would love to see important changes in how it is presented, for I feel that at present the congregation is asked to sit or stand passively while many thousands of words are poured over it, so many that not even the greatest saint could listen to each one of them. Despite this, the beautiful mystery of the death and resurrection of Jesus at the heart of the Mass constantly renews me.

I find beauty in an empty church at moments of quiet prayer, and greater beauty in the noise of a full church when people support each other by their very presence. I experience beauty when groups of people meet to understand and pray the scriptures, and when death is accepted in faith and a family gathers at a bedside.

I see great beauty in the lives of people such as Saint Mary MacKillop, who saw that the traditional church structures of her time in this country were not reaching the children who lived outside the cities. She threw convention to the winds, established a religious order unlike any other and reached out to those children across a vast and harsh land, never losing her marvellous blend of strength, gentleness and love.

I see parish communities supporting the St Vincent de Paul Society in reaching many of the most needy people in their midst. And I see international church agencies such as Caritas giving constant practical help to many people in many countries. As long as I don't simply pass my responsibilities off onto these agencies, I can feel that through them I am a small part of something far bigger than myself.

It is not easy to describe the beauty of the Catholic Church to those who have never seen it, but those who love that church experience it frequently. I have seen an abundance of ugly things in the church, but I constantly see the beauty as well, and I have no wish to cast aside this beauty.

THE JOURNEYS OF A MOTHER AND SON

The American President, Barack Obama, in the autobiographical sections of his books, tells a story of the journey I have described. His Kenyan father was raised a Muslim but had become an atheist. His American mother was an anthropologist who saw religion through the eyes of a scientist, but was also a most spiritually awakened person, with an unswerving instinct for kindness, charity and love. She worked hard to instil in her children the values of honesty, empathy, discipline, delayed gratification and hard work. She raged at poverty and injustice, and she possessed an abiding sense of wonder and reverence for life.[26]

She was suspicious of organised religion, and critical of every sign of hypocrisy within it.[27] Her language on this subject, however, could become the language of caricature, a language she would not have tolerated if used by another person on a subject such as the colour of a person's skin.

Both her personal experience and her preferences lay with the approach to life of an anthropologist, and her story is an example of the heart of a good and honest person leading her head in a certain direction as she engaged in the most ancient of struggles between belief and unbelief and knew that she could not live her whole life on the fence between them.

The very values that she had so assiduously cultivated in her son led him to community work among the people of South Chicago. There he continued to meet Christians who failed to

26 *The Audacity of Hope*, The Text Publishing Company, Melbourne, 2006, pp.204-205.
27 *Op.cit.*, p.203.

live up to their own ideals, but he also met a different side of the churches, particularly the black churches.[28] These churches could not afford to separate individual salvation from collective salvation, for they had to serve as the centre of the community's political, economic and social as well as spiritual life. Following the gospel had to mean literally feeding the hungry, clothing the naked and challenging the powerful.

He came to see that faith was more than just a comfort to the weary or a hedge against death, that faith did not mean the absence of doubt of turning one's back on the world.[29] These experiences began to cause his heart to lead his head in a direction different to that of his mother.

> I came to realize that without a vessel for my beliefs, without an unequivocal commitment to a particular community of faith, I would be consigned at some level to always remain apart, free in the way that my mother was free, but also alone in the same ways that she was ultimately alone.[30]

And so he finally accepted Christian baptism.

That the story concerns the President of the United States perhaps increases its interest, but does not change the fact that it is a universal story of humanity, repeated millions of times. Different temperaments, life experiences and desires led a mother and son in somewhat different directions on the fundamental questions of belief and unbelief. And yet there was nothing that they could not have discussed together, nothing on either side that need have caused the slightest hurt or alienation.

What they retained in common far outweighed any differences between them. They were, in fact, in complete

---

28 This story is told at greater length in Obama's earlier book, *Dreams from my Father*, The Text Publishing Company, Melbourne, 1995, see pp.131-295.

29 *Op.cit.,* p.207.

30 *Op.cit.,* p.206.

agreement on the question of the importance of spirituality and their differences concerned only the part more formal religion might play in the development of this spirituality. Indeed, the story shows just how close belief and unbelief can be to one another.

In this particular case the son, coming from a background of a form of unbelief, had to go through the process of seeing that caricatures could not express the whole truth. Typically for a person on such a journey, he expresses surprise and wonder at the idea that there could be religious bodies that actually care about this world, and at the thought that he would not have to suspend critical thinking or withdraw from the world. There is so much in this story with which other people would resonate.

THE CONFLICT BETWEEN SPIRITUALITY AND RELIGION

People who seek the spiritual would admit in theory that it is good to work with other people, both in seeking to respond to the desire for love within themselves and in seeking to help other people. People of today, however, have been so affected by the four body blows to religion I have spoken about that many believe that the religious communities available today are not the places in which to care for either themselves or others.

Furthermore, even those who believe in both God and church breathe the atmosphere of a secular society and conduct much of their ordinary lives according to its tenets. When such people come to church, they do not leave their complex inner worlds at the door, but bring the ambiguities right up to the altar.

For many, therefore, their experience has been of the ugliness rather than the beauty, and they feel that the noble goals have been too contaminated by less noble ones.

I have already referred to the most destructive of these less noble goals. There is the temptation for authorities to control the community through fear and the demand for conformity, with the result that spiritual energy cannot be properly accessed and expressed. There is the temptation for authorities to put too much of themselves into the religion, until the beauty and wonder of God has been tamed and it is a human rather than a divine religion that they are presenting.

There is the concern for the preservation and growth of the institution that the religious body has become, and particularly of its authority structures, siphoning off much important energy that could otherwise have been directed outwards towards others. There is the extolling of divine love at the cost of the denigration and suspicion of human love, let alone of sex. And there is the constant temptation for individuals to concentrate on their own longings for love while giving less emphasis to any reaching out to others.

We should always remember the thought of Voltaire that nothing so fosters atheism in a society as corruption, vice and pettiness in religious communities.

In matters such as these many people today believe that religious bodies have over the centuries gone to an extreme. And when people perceive that some powerful group has gone to an extreme, there is always the strong temptation for them to oppose this extreme by going to the opposite extreme. There are several ways in which this has happened today.

The result has been that spirituality and religion have been increasingly seen as opposed to each other, and in the process the two ideas have moved towards the extremes of their relative positions:

— In opposing the extremes of control imposed by the churches in the past, there is today a strong tendency to see spirituality as demanding the removal of all controls.
— Religion is said to be about certainties and obedience, while

spirituality is said to be about search and freedom.
- Religion is said to be about private morality, while spirituality is said to be about social justice.
- Religion is said to be about praying that God will solve the world's problems, while spirituality is said to be about doing the work to solve those problems ourselves.
- Religion is said to be about self-denial, while spirituality is said to be about a proper self-love.
- Religion is presented as anti-*eros*, anti-sex, anti-enjoyment, anti-this-world, while spirituality is presented as pro-*eros*, pro-sex, pro-enjoyment, pro-this-world.

Rolheiser perceptively describes the situation as that of a demanding-father Christianity and an adolescent modern culture, both resentful and failing to understand the other. We can look on like the wife-mother who loves both but does not know how to bridge the gap between them. She feels that each possesses part of the truth, but both fail to grasp what is most essential, for both fail to place love at the centre of their thinking, feeling and acting, and without this there can be no real solution.[31]

The first response must be to change "either...or" into "both...and". Religion and spirituality together must be about
- **both** accessing the maximum amount of energy within us **and** about learning to use that energy in the most effective manner by working with others;
- **both** putting in place the basic and necessary certainties without which our most fundamental desires could not be satisfied **and** providing abundant freedom for that sense of wonder and enquiry without which human life would shrivel;
- **both** matters of private morality, for this affects who I am

---

31 *Op.cit.*, p.37.

in my deepest being, **and** everything that comes under the heading of social justice, e.g. a concern for the good of all, a reaching out to the most needy and a sense of the part I play in the successes and failures of the whole human race through such things as the use of water or the generation of carbon dioxide;

— **both** prayer to God **and** action in the world, for action is the essential work of love looking outwards to other people, while prayer is the same love drawing strength from its source.

— **both** a proper sense of self-love and self-worth **and** a true sense of self-control and being in charge of my own life.

— **both** divine **and** human love, and this means that, while nothing in human life escapes the need for necessary control of energy, religion must learn to be far more pro-*eros*, pro-sex, pro-creativeness, pro-enjoyment, pro-this-world.

It follows that, if there is to be a re-uniting of spirituality and religion, both sides have much work to do.

CHANGE IN RELIGION

For religious bodies I suggest that the most profound changes of attitude required will be those of

— moving strongly away from all attempts to 'define' God towards "a stunned appreciation of an 'otherness' beyond the reach of language", with all the consequences that would flow from this;

— rejecting the angry god, not just in theory but also in practice, from <u>every</u> aspect of life, and this includes the complete rejection of the use of fear as a means of coercing the actions of people;

— radically confronting the glaring scandals within their own ranks, especially the abomination of sexual abuse of minors, before daring to tell anyone else how to act on any other subject;

— stressing , through actions far more than words, the mutual interdependence of meeting our own needs and responding to the needs of others, or in other words, showing that the only way to gain the next world is by being passionately involved in this world and seeking to transform it;

— stressing the complementarity of divine and human love and seeing all the positives in *eros*;

— moving from a stress on the need for external control of energy to the fostering of the maximum energy possible within individuals, while at the same time helping people to find within themselves the necessary control of that energy;

— the consequent passing of as much power as possible from higher authority structures within the institution to more local structures and to individuals;

— stressing the consequent need for people to think, search, question and take responsibility for their actions.

CHANGE IN THE COMMUNITY

On the other hand, two major requests must also be made to the whole community today. The first is that people seek to fight against the seduction of immediate satisfaction that so abounds in the Western world and try instead to respond to the deepest desires within themselves.

The second is that people seek to move beyond the sense of individualism that so dominates the same Western world, and appreciate better how individuals need community.

These two questions require further comment, for any true spirituality needs to be strongly involved in all the major issues of the times. I believe that these more public issues are so important that my personal spirituality cannot exist without them.

THE INDUSTRIAL REVOLUTION

In a village in the time before the Industrial Revolution people worked with their own hands at jobs they knew and felt competent in, and so had a sense of achievement and of controlling their own destiny. They knew and were known by their neighbours, and patterns of mutual support were developed. There were all too many examples of discrimination and dysfunction, but society had a basic coherence that sustained it.

In a city after the Industrial Revolution, by contrast, people found that the factories could not function unless they were planned to a degree that reduced the status of each worker on an assembly line to that of a tiny part in a big process. In the large cities and factories, as a consequence, they came to feel that few people knew, needed or respected them, or even cared whether they lived or died.

Thus people felt alienated from the society in which they lived, no longer part of it. Two World Wars, the Great Depression, the Cold War with its threat of nuclear holocaust and the growth of technology all tended to reinforce these attitudes.

There was bound to be a rebellion against this feeling of helplessness and alienation and it occurred in the 1960s. The movement exploded in forces as wildly diverse as independence from colonial regimes, the civil rights movements, the Beatles, the first stirrings of the emancipation of women, flower power and the drug culture, and the Second Vatican Council.

It reflected a spontaneous need to reassert human dignity and place people above machines. There was a universal urge to assert, "I am a person, I matter, I am important. I am not just a number on a card, a cipher in a computer file."

It was a good movement, for in the Industrial Revolution the dignity of the individual had been trampled on. At the same time, it was a tumultuous movement and we should not be surprised if there were also some defects. I suggest that there were two major defects.

Attacking the Lesser Targets
The first was that the movement spent most of its enormous energy on the less important targets because they were easier to attack. It is easier to attack the personal targets of parents, politicians, policemen, priests and teachers than it is to attack machines, ignorance, inertia, poverty and war, the more impersonal and more powerful causes of alienation.

If it must be admitted that there was and is plenty to attack in the personal targets, it must also be said that this massive movement has done little to overcome the more serious causes of alienation. Indeed, it may be argued that the persons being attacked are precisely the people we will most need if we are to overcome the deeper problems. Thus many of the dehumanising effects of the Industrial Revolution are still with us.

Because we have become a global society, the causes of alienation arising from the Industrial Revolution now concern powerful, world-wide forces. To mention some of the major ongoing fears, there is widespread anxiety about
— nuclear, chemical and biological weapons;
— international terrorism;
— long-term conflict between Islam and the West;
— over-population;
— fear of a killer pandemic in a crowded world of international travel;
— the constant unrest caused by the massive inequality in the world's wealth;
— floods of refugees no one will accept;

- the genocidal madness that too often erupts;
- the cheapness of human life in the eyes of too many people and the endless violations of human dignity that flow from this;
- global warming, pollution and exploitation of the world's finite resources;
- machines and computers causing further unemployment;
- greed causing an international financial crisis;
- the lack of power of the United Nations to achieve its goals;
- the inability of nations to develop an economic system that is fair to all peoples on the planet;
- the inability to deal with tyrants and political instability.

Before forces such as these the attacks on individual persons or groups of persons can seem petty and irrelevant. If we hope for a new vision for this millennium, we must confront the hard targets, and in doing this we must seek to use to the full the contribution of parents, politicians, police, priests and teachers rather than simply attack their defects.

I and We

The second major defect was that the movement caused a considerable loss of the sense of community, of our need for each other. In reacting against the way in which individuals had been repressed by the Industrial Revolution, it went to the opposite extreme and over-emphasised the primacy of the individual, setting the individual against the community as though it were the enemy.

The balance between the individual good and the common good is always one of the most difficult problems facing any society. In the Industrial Revolution the individual good was largely crushed, while the 1960s movement suffered from the common human defect of going from one extreme to the opposite extreme, and of over-emphasising the individual at the expense of the community.

There has, therefore, been a strong tendency to value personal freedom above social responsibilities, and to make personal choice an ultimate criterion for public life. Precisely because the dehumanising effects of the Industrial Revolution have not been overcome, this move to emphasise the individual is still enormously powerful.

THE NEED FOR COMMUNITY

Today, on the other hand, the world has suddenly been presented with new and massive problems. There is global warming, a problem that could lead to an unliveable planet unless we take prompt and strong action. And there is the unprecedented financial crisis that overtook the world in 2008-2009. If the Western world is beginning to come out of this crisis, poorer countries will suffer from its devastating effects for many years to come, and we have not yet taken serious steps to overcome the causes of this crisis.

These problems are so big that they have created a completely new situation requiring new solutions and even a quite new set of values.

The two problems have already become so interlinked that it will be impossible to solve one without at the same time addressing the other. A response to global warming cannot be simply put on hold until all financial problems have been resolved, and it is equally impossible to tackle global warming without sound national economies.

When taken together, they constitute, it may be argued, one of the greatest problems the world as a whole has ever had to face. There are no precedents for this problem or for how to go about resolving it.

I am neither a scientist nor a financier, so I have nothing to offer at those practical levels. There I look for leadership from a consensus of those who are experts in these fields and from governments, which must take responsibility for implementing plans.

My concern here is different. Earlier in this book I spoke of a meeting to discuss the drug problem in the state where I live. I said that different people spoke of it as a physical and mental health problem, a social problem, a law and order problem and an education problem, but insufficient attention was given to the fact that it is *first and foremost a spiritual problem*. I felt that, unless serious attention is given to the spiritual problem, it is unlikely that efforts in more practical fields will be as effective as we would wish.

I believe that the twin problems of global warming and finance are also and in first place a moral and a spiritual crisis, and that, if we do not attend to these basic aspects of the problem, many of our practical efforts will be wasted.

Global warming is a moral crisis because the kind of world we are leaving to our children is ultimately a moral question. After all, how can we say that we love our children if we are at the same time rushing ahead to create an unliveable world for them? And it is a spiritual crisis because it involves both our collective response to the deepest desires within us and the whole relationship between ourselves and the planet we live on.

The financial crisis is also both moral and spiritual, for its greatest effects will always be on people in poorer countries who were in no way responsible for the crisis and are least able to cope with it.

Both the financial crisis and global warming have also been moral and spiritual in their origins. This is obvious in the financial crisis, as evidence has poured in of a culture of greed, the paying of obscene salaries and the lending of money that didn't really exist until a house of cards fell to the ground.

While much blame must go to the leaders of this movement, it is not possible to ignore the contribution made by the wider community, for the actions of financial institutions could not have taken place without a widespread culture of endless consumption, unlimited growth and easy money. If a seemingly attractive house of cards was being built, many people wanted their part of it.

In overcoming the financial crisis, we cannot simply go back to the previous world of consumption. That culture must be left behind and a more sober culture must take its place. If spirituality is understood as the desire to rise towards higher goals, then the financial crisis involves a spiritual crisis. Its solution must involve a conscious and universal desire to rise above the culture of consumerism towards one based on reality rather than a house of cards, on sober and sustainable consumption and on a concern for the good of the whole community rather than for self alone.

Similar comments can be made about the crisis of global warming. The world has existed for billions of years, and yet in a time as brief as two hundred years human beings have brought it close to a point of catastrophe. We have filled it with pollution, of which carbon dioxide is only one element, to such an extent that only with great difficulty can we restore it, and even then only if we can truly find the will to do so.

The most basic cause has been the lack of a proper spirituality concerning the world we inhabit, for the crisis is the result of a headlong race towards prosperity without concern for the effects we might be having on the planet.

Stewardship is the careful and responsible management of something entrusted to one's care, and we, the human race, are the stewards of God's creation. We were not content with this, however, and convinced ourselves that we were the owners, not stewards, so that dominion replaced stewardship.

If no one is asked to say, "I did this", we are all asked to say, "We did this, and I made my contribution, for I was part of the culture of consumption. Whether some other people made a bigger contribution than I did is irrelevant, for we all contributed."

If no one is asked to say, "I will overcome this problem", we are all asked to say, "We will overcome it, and I will make my contribution, for I will be part of the new relationship with the planet. Whether some other people make a smaller contribution than I do is irrelevant, for we must all contribute as much as we can."

Here, too, we cannot simply go back to the world of consumption, profligate use of the world's resources and consequent pollution, but must forge a new, more sober and more realistic world.

MONEY, SEX AND POWER

Money, sex and power have always been three of the biggest temptations to human beings, and they are present today, both in the financial crisis and in global warming. Early in its history the Christian church responded to these temptations with the ideas of poverty, chastity and obedience, but in the forms they took these will always be only for the few. A middle ground is urgently needed, and I suggest that it may be summed up in the ideas of simplicity, fidelity and service.[32]

Simplicity could replace the relentless pursuit of money on the one hand and the negative connotations of the word

32 See Jim Wallis, *Seven Ways to Change the World, Reviving Faith and Politics*, Lion Hudson, Oxford, 2008, pp.223-225.

'poverty' on the other. An attitude of simplicity would ask us just how big a house and television set we really <u>need</u>, as distinct from merely desire, and just how necessary are many of the things we can so easily convince ourselves that we must have. It would look to a sustainable world and those things that all people in every country could reasonably possess without harming the planet. It would seek to remind people that, if some possess far more than this reasonable amount, the planet will be harmed and others will necessarily possess less than is necessary.

<u>Fidelity</u> would replace the relentless pursuit of sex with the desire to unite sex and love so that they support each other. It would seek to give greater stability to marriage and family, and hence to society itself. It would be aware that the word "fidelity" means far more than just the avoidance of sexual infidelity. Counterbalancing the other two elements of money and power, this element stresses the need for better interpersonal relationships and a better sense of community if we are to overcome our problems.

<u>Service</u> stresses the fact that all power is power to serve. This is the sole basis for power and the sole reason that justifies its existence. A leader needs power, but solely so that the community may be served, never solely so that the leader may be glorified or feel powerful. It is legitimate to seek power, but only if the basic intention is to serve the community. The idea of service does not do away with the pursuit of legitimate power, but places the emphasis on its responsibilities rather than its privileges.

Simplicity, fidelity and service, replacing the endless pursuit of money, sex and power, are attitudes of mind that are surely essential to a new spirituality for a sustainable planet and a prosperous humanity.

INDIVIDUAL AND COMMUNITY

There has been a serious measure of international cooperation on the financial crisis, though I believe it has been only at the pragmatic level of fixing the more obvious faults of financial systems and introducing a measure of cooperation in fiscal and monetary policy.

The defect in this action is that it is still based on the idea that we can soon return to the culture of consumption that we had before. I believe that we must seriously question this assumption. We should not attempt to resolve practical problems without seriously addressing the spiritual problem that lies beneath them.

On the question of global warming, there are many individuals who are convinced that decisive action should have taken place many years ago, and that the longer it is left, the more difficulties we create for ourselves. Many have made serious adjustments to their own private lifestyles. In other words, a significant spiritual revolution has taken place within the minds and hearts of these individuals. They feel frustrated, however, that they are so few and that there is so little that they can do as individuals to cope with a vast world-wide problem.

Many governments are also well aware of the problems, but they face two difficulties. In the first place, in a democracy a government cannot afford to leave the people too far behind on a major and highly expensive matter or it will quickly find itself out of office at the next election.

The government is therefore caught in a dilemma. On the one side, there is the amount of change demanded by global warming, while on the other side there is the amount of change that the government believes the electorate will tolerate before it rebels and votes against it. So far there has been a considerable, even a vast, gap between these two amounts of change.

Unfortunately, opposition parties seem to engage in political point-scoring even on this issue, for in politics winning government always seems to be more important than saving the planet. I am not aware of a single country where there has been a true bipartisan approach. The result is much rhetoric, but action that falls a long way short of what is needed.

The second problem is that every government knows that only a concerted world-wide response will be adequate, so no government wants to introduce highly painful measures within its own country, only to find that it is acting alone. The world-wide response is, therefore, taking place at the pace of the slowest nations, particularly the powerful nations.

In the past the only thing that has created both bipartisan action within countries and concerted action between countries has been the imminent threat of war. It was, for instance, the threat of the Second World War that created the consensus and the hard work to bring the world out of the Great Depression of the 1930s.

Does this mean that we will not take adequate action until we perceive such an imminent and massive threat? Will we need some cataclysmic and truly shocking event in nature to convince us that global warming is real? At the moment, this seems all too likely. But by then will it be too late?

A SPIRITUALITY OF COMMUNITY

The stress in recent years on the essential dignity of every individual is good and necessary. The balance between individual and community was often lost in the Industrial Revolution, as the individual was subjected to the machine to such an extent that far too many individuals were harmed, not helped by what was called "progress".

But now the situation has changed dramatically and there is a profound and urgent need for people to work together to confront the twin problems of global warming and the financial crisis. In this new situation the supremacy of the individual over the community is working against us.

We must not go back to the situation of the Industrial Revolution or lose any of the gains that have been made in human rights. But Western society did move from one extreme to the other extreme, and it is now time to find a better balance between the two.

It has been well said that we need to move from a society that is "egocentric contractual" to one that is "sociocentric organic". In the first, society consists of a large number of independent individuals who then agree or contract certain limited things that they will do in common. In the second, society is a living organism in which the individual can no more live independently of other people than the hand can live without the rest of the body.[33]

We need to act in this way also because we have come to realise that the planet we live on cannot be treated as no more than an object of our contracts, but is itself an organism, and we must learn to live as part of that organism.

Precisely because we are spiritual beings, we are defined through our personal relationships with the people around us. The more authentically we live these relationships, the more we will grow as individuals. In a good family the individuality of each member is encouraged rather than suppressed and, in the same way, in a whole society each person grows, not by insisting on a rugged individualism and a separation from other people, but by relating to the other members of that society.[34]

33 See Elizabeth A Johnson, *Quest for the Living God, Mapping Frontiers in the Theology of God,* Continuum Press, New York, 2007, p.143.
34 Pope Benedict XVI, Encyclical Letter *Caritas in Veritate,* Libreria Editrice Vaticana, Vatican City, 2009, pp.104-105.

In order to be effective in confronting global warming and the financial crisis, a better balance between individual and community must be combined with a spiritual revolution, in which we collectively go back to the deepest desires within us and decide how they can best be satisfied for the human race as a whole.

This must involve a hard look at the world in which we live, hard decisions concerning what is possible in sustainable development for the whole world and the seeking of some consensus on what things are most essential in responding to the fundamental desires within us.

If spirituality concerns the conscious attempt to rise towards higher goals, then we must, by studying our fundamental desires, form clearer collective ideas about what those higher goals are in the world of the twenty-first century, and how we, as one human race, can move towards them. The entire world needs to ask the question, "What is the most loving thing to do here?"

In writing about these matters I hope that I have shown that some deep desires of my own are involved. If my spirituality is to be part of my real world, then I must live it out in the midst of these global issues. If I am to have a personal spirituality, I must have some sense of a spirituality for the world.

To go further into these matters, however, would involve a new book rather than a brief addition to this one. As I bring this book to a conclusion, therefore, allow me to return to the question of my personal spirituality.

A CONCLUSION FOR MY OWN LIFE

In everything I do or say or think I am seeking to respond to "love's urgent longings". These longings are essential to my very identity as a human being and individual person. They have led me to a renewed belief in God and to a renewed belief in my need for community.

I know that values, especially those that require effort, need to be constantly reinforced by habit and, indeed, by some form of ritual, if they are to remain strong. For much of my life it has been in the Catholic Church that I have found this habit and ritual, and it has been one of the better things in that church.

At the same time, I have also seen great ugliness there and felt a powerful need for profound change. I therefore feel a serious, deep seated ambivalence about the church and probably always will. Inevitably it will at one time overwhelm me with beauty and inspiration, and at another time so disgust me that I feel as physically sick as I have over the sexual abuse crisis.

If my love relationship with God grows weaker, I can always hope to renew it. On the other hand, I have such ambivalence about the church that I fear that my relationship with it will always be like that of a son towards a mother who has done many good motherly things but who has also been too controlling, wanting me always to remain the good little obedient boy I once was and not allowing me to grow up. Any level of independence from her I have finally achieved has been hard won and I will not surrender it, for my own growth, maturity and integrity are at stake.

I will always find her decisions and actions concerning sexual abuse abhorrent, and this means that I will never again have the same respect for her I once had. I have told her what I think; she is angry at my criticism, and it is a serious block between us. As long as she maintains that I cannot question anything and everything that might have contributed to abuse, the block will remain. As a result, I can never again be confident that, in any decision that might reflect on her own image, she will act justly and lovingly. If I can dive into the sea of belief in God and in Jesus Christ, I find that I will never again be able to dive into the sea of belief in everything the Catholic Church says or does, and accept that world without question.

And yet, despite all the ambivalence and unhealthy elements in my relationship with her, I still find that I can not simply walk away and abandon her. If I could never be serene in the world of atheism, I could also never be serene in a world where I had totally excluded her from my life and found no replacement. She is still the only spiritual mother I have ever had, and there are too many memories, too many shared experiences. I can never forget the love we once had and, despite the tensions, I still feel affection for her.

In terms of the two desires that are inherent in all love, I still profoundly want all that is good for her, but I am so ambivalent about her that I no longer want her to be an important part of every aspect of my life in the way I once did. I must accept that our love will now be one of those imperfect and rather sad loves that many people have to settle for after dreams have died.

And so, after all this thinking I find that, at the stage of life I have reached, my conclusion is no more noble than the pragmatic one that I do not have either the heart or the energy to throw away the good with the bad and start all over again.

I most certainly do not wish to abandon Jesus Christ, but I also have little desire to transfer to some other Christian church, for that would be like changing mothers and I have no expectations that other communities would be better. Above all, as I said at the very beginning of this book, I have no wish to do no more than reject whatever I have had and replace it with nothing.

Within the Catholic Church I have learned how to avoid many ugly things and how to find many beautiful things. In one sense, to move outside the church and criticise it would be an easier path, but I find that I am still prepared to follow the harder path of staying and trying to change it from within. I am prepared to do this because I believe that this vast, world-wide community, despite all its massive problems, is still capable of inspiring immense good.

I have concluded, therefore, that, unless I am pushed out, I shall continue to try to find my way to God within that ugly and beautiful church. If I am pushed out, it would be a cause of great sadness to me, but I have to add that it would not be the total catastrophe it would once have been, and I would seek to adjust.

I am not at the end of my journey, but this is the point I have currently reached. I shall continue to speak the truth as I see it, for this integrity is essential to me, and perhaps this is what God is calling me to be.

Over the past few years I have found an abundance of people within the church who are going through exactly the same struggles as myself, and in their company I find much support, though I shall always long for the fuller support of the entire church community.

I have said that in these matters we are all guided by the two forces of our personal experience and what we want to believe, and I feel that this is exactly what I am doing. This is where my unique personal experience has led me and I find that, at least in the messy and imperfect world in which I must exist, this is what I want to believe. Readers will have their own experience and, deep within themselves, they will have to discover what it is that they most want to believe.

Of course, as well as living in an imperfect church, I must also work in an imperfect world. And yet I have to confess that it is in this confusing church and world that I have done my most important growing.

When I think back on my life, I sometimes grew through tasks that I consciously set before myself and worked hard to carry out. But I would have to add that I did far more growing through the things that happened to me from outside, things I did not plan or want, things that tested me to the limit and made me somehow descend to the depths within myself.

And these things forcibly reminded me of my own imperfection, inadequacy and brokenness. I, a broken person, must live and work in a broken church and a broken world, and it is precisely this that has greatly contributed to my growth.

Why God created the world the way it is I do not know. But, despite all the difficulties, I am glad I was born. And I find that I still have both the desire and the energy to try to take hold of this messy self and messy church and messy world and do whatever is within my power to make them better.